Get a Life:

Sane Wisdom for an Insane World

Other Titles by Loretta LaRoche

The Best of Loretta LaRoche (4-CD set)
Parenting with Humor and Optimism (DVD)

Relax: You Only Have A Few Minutes Left: Using The Power of Humor to Overcome Stress in Your Life and Work (book)

Kick Up Your Heels... Before You're Too Short to Wear Them
How to Live a Long, Healthy, Juicy Life (book)

Life is Short – Wear Your Party Pants
Ten Simple Truths That Lead to an Amazing Life (Available as a book, 2-CD set, and a DVD)

Squeeze the Day: 365 Ways to Bring JOY and JUICE into Your Life (book)

All of the above are available at your local bookstore, or may be ordered by visiting:

www.lorettalaroche.com
www.thebookshack.net

Get a Life: *Sane Wisdom for an Insane World* is a compilation of columns written by Loretta LaRoche, an international stress management consultant and humorist. They were written over the last several years and are focused on societal observations that are often absurd and stress provoking. Loretta offers not only her viewpoint, but also practical, optimistic and fun ways to deal with our daily lives.

Copyright© 2013 by Humor Potential, Inc.

All rights reserved.

Published in the United States by

Humor Potential, Inc.

ISBN :

978-1492705338

Printed in the United States of America
by
Create Space

Designed by Erika Christensen
Edited by Tory Axford and Erika Christensen
Plymouth, Massachusetts

For my loyal readers.
May you embrace each day,
be inspired,
and learn how to laugh at yourself.

With appreciation to all who made this
project possible,
including myself,
my son Erik and his wife Dawn,
my editor Tory, my designer and
granddaughter Erika
and many thanks to my partner Kenny
for his love and support

Chapter 1

HURRY UP and *Slow Down*

"The trouble with the rat race is that even if you win, you're still a rat."

~Lily Tomlin

There are no do-overs in life

I am constantly amused by how impatient everyone has become. No one wants to wait for anything.

Merchants are trying to provide services as quickly as possible, and yet the public still frets and fumes when a burger and fries takes more than five minutes to serve.

At first, the idea of fast food was embraced with great gusto. We were enthralled by the concept of getting an entire meal in less than twenty minutes. However, since life has become a *to-do list*, every retailer has gotten on the bandwagon to provide services to get you what you need as quickly as possible.

No stone has been left unturned. You can get your cleaning in less than twenty-four hours, even though you may have twenty years of debris embedded in the material. Your eyeglass prescription can be filled in twenty seconds. Cholesterol screenings take five minutes, while you are training your dog not to poop on the rug.

You can have your thighs reshaped during lunch and your breasts lifted while you're having dinner. If that's not to your liking, you can have a mini-tuck at your local gas station while you're filling your tank.

You can do psychotherapy while you're in your car driving to work. You just pick up your therapist and take him with you. He picks your brain while you pick on the other drivers on the road for not driving fast enough to suit your accelerated mind.

Televisions now have screens within screens which allow us to watch two programs at the same time, just in case we have some free time while the primary program is lackluster. There seems to be a universal clicking as individuals try frantically to get through messages they feel are boring and useless. Why bother listening to anything that might sound familiar even though, at some point, there might be new information? After all, we don't want to waste any time. We are too important. Let's hurry up and get this mundane stuff over with so we can get to the important stuff.

Like what? The reality is that whatever we do at any given moment is our life. There will be no repeat performances.

We're all becoming invested in the hurry-up-sickness mentality.

The bottom line is that not everyone is a paramedic. Unless you are, stop acting like you're part of a Grey's Anatomy segment when you're just going through a toll booth.

Take a deep breath and pay for the person in back of you. It could extend your life.

Gotta get back to Lala-Land

Remember when you were a kid and you got into your heavy staring? Your mother would say, "Come back! Where are you? In Lala-Land?"

By now you've probably buried or dismissed this wonderful place that can help us illicit inner peace and harmony. But as children, we daydreamed often and with great ease. It's because we were so clearly focused on our intent and where we were at any given moment.

If children see a kite, balloon, or bird, they will zero in on it like sonar and track it with complete absorption.

As parents, we often scurry after a small child who is following something that has become the object of his interest. It's as if he has become one with this object.

This becomes harder and harder to do as our minds become more and more cluttered with adult demands. How often have you sat down for a few minutes to chill out when you started hearing those nagging little inner voices asking, "Why are you resting? You know you don't have time for this! Get up, don't just sit there. You have lots to do. Keep going!"

Children don't have these voices yet. That's why we have to keep telling them to clean their rooms, pick up their toys, and watch where they are going. They're so wrapped up in their delightful, adventurous activities, and so totally involved, that it is no wonder the universal mantra for parents is "Please look at me, I'm talking to you." We hope that if they look at us, it will break the spell.

We can all learn to be spellbound again, to connect to that earlier experience my mother called Lala-Land. It is not about writing one more report or finishing one more project, but rather it is about becoming more in touch with the universe.

I find that my garden draws me into this other world. When I'm there, I transcend time and space and let go of cares and concerns. There is nothing that puts things into perspective more than a squirrel that is trying for the hundredth time to get into a bird feeder with a cone-shaped top. Time after time it simply flips off and falls to the ground; yet, without fail, it tries again. It appears that the frustration is part of the game. For us, frustration is part of the struggle.

I also realize there is a simpler, more majestic world, where phones don't ring and no deadlines exist. Not one bird in my yard has voicemail or an e-mail address. It appears that as we evolve, we also dissolve.

Take time to stare at the clouds, stars, moon, flowers, people (politely, of course), kids playing, animals cavorting – anything that allows you to go to that wonderful place where there is no time and where time stands still.

Let's stop turning food into medicine

When I was growing up, eating did not feel like we were in a control group for the National Institute of Health. You ate what was put in front you and it didn't matter if you liked it or not! Your parents would remind you that they weren't running a restaurant.

Smell was also very important. The women in the family, and my grandfather who loved making spaghetti, spent many hours getting the smells right. No matter when you walked into the house, you were smothered in odors that wafted throughout, permeating every inch. They often lasted for weeks, especially when inspired by garlic and onions.

Although we are still seduced by looks and tastes, the primary discussions about food appear to be about the benefits we will get once they get into our system. There isn't a magazine printed, no matter what the subject matter, that does not contain something about the pluses or minuses of whatever you're eating.

It doesn't matter if you leave the country, since the food disclosure epidemic has reached the four corners of the universe. I imagine somewhere in Tibet there is a periodical called Monk Mastery that encourages eating boiled yak in order to chant more profusely.

Ironically, nothing about the positive side effects one receives through eating certain foods is new. We've all heard "eat your carrots, you'll see better." How often will we be told that spinach makes you strong, milk helps your bones, and oatmeal gets you through the day?

The problem was that it all sounded too simplistic and the message was delivered by parents who were not in lab coats. Many of us did it just because they said, "Do it. I'm the boss."

Almost everyone is now a professor of nutrition. Carrots are no longer just carrots; they are the vehicle to transport beta carotene. Fruits and vegetables can lower blood pressure and help prevent cancer and macular degeneration, as well as reduce the likelihood of getting prostate cancer. Fiber is a natural laxative. Orange juice contains potassium, folic acid, and vitamin C. Fatty fish, like salmon, contain omega-3 fatty acids, which are good for your heart, and soy can help with menopause.

I imagine that soon we will find that eating artichokes will help us vacuum faster, and perhaps mangos will remove hair from our upper lips.

It is highly unlikely that you can have either breakfast, lunch, or dinner with someone today who does not somehow know something about how you will either live or die by the food you're eating.

I think we've gone too far! How about going back to simple enjoyment? Or maybe we should start gnawing on some two-by-fours and eat nails; then we might end up being our own deck. Now there is a benefit.

Think fast!
We're living our lives at the pace of a race

Why is everyone so obsessed with convenience? Everywhere I go, signs exclaim: Fast! Easy! No waiting!

People hardly have to get out of their cars anymore to buy or do anything. We can do our banking, grab a burger, and pick up our dry-cleaning all while sitting on our butts.

Let's face it: even if we do get out of our cars, day-to-day life has become unbelievably easy. We try to park next to the entrance of the store. If we can't, we circle the parking lot, stalking anyone who looks like he or she might be going toward a space. It can get nasty too, especially when two cars are tracking the same spot.

The same impatience can be seen elsewhere. Burger King had an issue where they had to reevaluate their service due to complaints that they were not fast enough. It was in the seven minute range and, after efficiency experts were done, customers could have it their way and be on their way in around five-and-a-half minutes. This obsession with speed speaks to the hurry sickness permeating everyone's lives.

Apparently no one has time anymore to travel from store to store, so now it's possible to purchase everything from underwear to plane tickets in the same mega-store. God forbid we should have to travel a few extra miles or walk a few extra steps. The result of this need for expedience has created a host of problems.

Obesity is at an all-time high, not just from overeating but also from under-doing. Many people live like invalids these days. Looking for the remote has become the only exercise some people get. This hurry-up-and-wait-on-me attitude has resulted in adult behavior that resembles a two-year-old's tantrums.

What is the point?

It is impossible to relish life and all its precious moments when our goal is to escape them so that we can get on to the next moment.

So, what's the answer?

I believe we need to reflect back to a time when people viewed life as a stroll instead of a sprint.

My grandfather turned visits to the local merchants into chat-fests. He engaged everyone he met and had a great time with them. He often walked to and from stores carrying heavy bundles. Every day was an opportunity to connect with people laugh, and enjoy life. This is not a difficult concept to incorporate into our lives.

When life becomes too convenient, we get lazy, diminishing our resilience. Learn to embrace waiting. Instead of fretting and fuming, breathe deeply and count your blessings.

Here and now will be gone soon enough

At the beginning of August, I went to the local nursery to buy some plants for my garden. As I pulled up, I noticed *them*! I began to feel overwhelming anxiety as I realized that the mums were out and waiting to be planted.

You're probably scratching your head thinking, "She's totally lost it."

Well, my friends, I don't think that I've gone off the deep end, but I sure do think we as a culture have. Chrysanthemums, which are a colorful fall plant, are simply another metaphor for making us lose the ability to enjoy life in the here and now.

The beginning of August now means getting ready for fall. Some stores are now starting to feature Halloween costumes and candy. By late September we'll start to see Christmas displays and by mid-December the Valentine cards will be out.

Why the rush? Or, more importantly, what's the point?

When I was growing up, and, trust me, I know I'm beginning to sound more and more like my mother, no one lived life with such a futuristic mindset. About two weeks before Halloween, you started thinking about your outfit. No one had to buy anything because there was nothing to buy. And, quite frankly, my mother wouldn't have bought it anyway. Her only suggestion was to go find an old sheet and be a ghost. After that it was up to me. If I didn't have an imagination, I copied someone else.

Apples, pennies, and homemade cookies were the treats of the day, and everybody was excited to go home, empty their sacks, and count their stuff. Once in a while, I got a nickel or a dime and thought I was rich.

I don't think today's children would feel rich. And it doesn't have anything to do with money. Our spirits and souls, and those of the next generation, are suffering from poverty – a poverty that comes from not being able to savor and enjoy the here and now, but rather think that the next experience will be better.

Our consumer-driven society seduces us and our children with these messages every day. Why thoroughly enjoy summer when you can get anxious about fall and getting new clothing for school?

No, wait: forget getting adjusted to school and the beauty of an Indian summer; start twitching over getting your Halloween pumpkins. Then, the minute you bring home your pumpkin, you'd better start getting out your Christmas decorations.

Don't rob yourself of the present. Try to live consciously each day. This is not an easy concept to grasp, particularly in a culture that validates life at warp speed.

Interrupt the need to always advance the day by reminding yourself that you are joyfully in the moment. It is, after all is said and done, the only moment you can be sure of.

We should heed men's fashion attitudes

I went on a mission to find a pair of black pumps: a shoe that could be worn with a number of outfits and that had class, style, and was, most importantly, comfortable. It had been a while since I'd been in a shoe store, so I was shocked to see that the era of pointy toes and stiletto heels had returned to haunt the female foot.

Every decade some unhappy, unfulfilled fashion designer decides to impose pain and discomfort on women. Of course, we are all being held prisoner to this cruel hoax: let's try to seduce women into believing that they all look better when they force their feet in shoes from Hell. But somehow a hallucinogenic drug must be given out before women try them on. Why else would someone wear something that forces her foot in into wedges and then makes her walk on four inch heels that resemble pencils?

Have we gone mad?

There have been numerous articles on how women's feet have become deformed from ill-fitting footwear and how back pain can be a direct result of wearing shoes that throw off your balance. And yet the beat goes on.

What fascinates me is how women endure any amount of discomfort to look sexy and feminine. No man in his right mind would go to such extremes to look attractive. When was the last time you heard a man tell you he couldn't wait to go home and take his shoes off, or anything else he was wearing, because it was killing him?

Their clothes come off for other reasons, but not because they're in pain.

Why have we returned to this ridiculous and foolhardy trend? Well, let's face it: it doesn't take a brain surgeon to figure it out. They create something new so you'll go out and buy more shoes, because you've been made to believe you're foolish and outdated with what you have. Men don't seem to buy into that concept. They'll wear something until it disintegrates, simply because it is comfortable. Try to tell him it's out of style and he looks at you like you've lost your mind. That's because guys don't stand around and discuss what they've got on, where they bought it, or how much they paid for it. They simply don't care.

I think it's time we took a little step in that direction. It doesn't mean we have to look like someone out of American Gothic, but let's use some common sense. Our feet have to last, and hopefully in good condition, so we can get to where we want to go. A journey of a thousand miles begins with a comfortable pair of shoes.

Yes, you can have too much stuff

I am sure there have been times you heard someone say: "I just found this amazing silk jacket. It cost only $95. I saw it last week for $300. What a deal!"

Now, let's be real here. Is anyone naïve enough to believe that jacket ever was worth $300?

It's probably worth about $50, and was insanely overpriced before. Now, it's only mildly overpriced, but we feel as if we've saved money when what we've really done is buy another thing we probably don't need.

I'll bet, too, there were many times you heard: "You can't have too many black pants." Oh, yeah? Who says?

When will you know that you have too many black pants? When God speaks to you and hurls lightning bolts into your closet? When the pants come bursting out of your closet on their own? Of course, you can have too much of anything – especially if you're charging the items on credit cards and giving up other things that can enrich your soul. If you have ever thought, "I just can't have too many of ..." whatever it is you like, then shopping just may be your addiction.

I hear friends say; "I found a bag at Marshall's for $20 that I saw three weeks ago at Neiman Marcus for $50! It took three hours of looking around, but I found something great!"

Is that really a good way to spend a day? It's amazing how many people actually make pilgrimages to outlet malls so they can rummage through mounds of stuff.

Take a look in your closet. If you're anything like me, you probably end up wearing some of the same stuff over and over and over. The rest of it sits there because you probably bought it in a moment of emotional need.

I often think that if I had invested half the money I spent on clothing I hardly ever wore, I just might have a sizable nest egg. Even if you don't want to save it, there are better alternatives for your money than being a slave to the god of shopping.

The next time you think you need another item of ready-to-wear, consider spending the money on tickets to a Broadway show or on a weekend away to some exotic place you've never been to before.

Consider taking a friend out to lunch, or sending flowers to a parent. If you really want to stretch yourself, donate the money to a worthy cause so someone else's face lights up with delight.

We have so many options on how and where to spend our hard-earned money. Remember, you can't take any of this stuff with you. I've never seen a tombstone that said, "Here lies Jane Doe. She had seventy-five blouses and forty pairs of pants."

Keep small stuff in perspective

In one of my recent stress management workshops I met a woman who was terminally serious about her towels. Towels are as important to her as the economy is to Alan Greenspan.

She loves her towels. Beautiful stitching and perfect color-coordinated towels hanging in the kitchen or bathroom is a work of art. She chooses her towels the way chef Julia Child chooses tomatoes – each has to be the right color, texture and thickness. Her towels are folded and placed just so, to look fluffy and inviting.

The proper arrangement and selection of her towels means a lot to her. It makes a clear statement about how she feels about her home, and her personal taste and style.

The problem: her husband. He doesn't have the same aesthetics or priorities. A towel, to him, is something you wipe your hands on. It was clear that this has been seething inside of her for years as she relayed her tale in the workshop. Suddenly, her husband was Attila the Hun because he used one of the "guest" towels to dry his face.

"My God," the wife said, "how could he show so little consideration?"

She once caught him using one of the "good" kitchen towels to wipe up a spill on the floor.

Stories like this amaze me – they remind me of how easy it is for most of us to take something so seemingly insignificant as a pimple on an elephant's butt and turn it into a nuclear conflict.

Of course those little things (like towels) are not what is really bothering us. They are manifestations of larger issues in our lives. We need to take a look at the amount of energy we spend feeling bad, anxious and conflicted, and look for the real source.

If it is something small, then why are we bothering? When we obsess over the small stuff, it's because on some level we are not getting the love and nurturing we need to feel complete.

As children we were cuddled and held to ease fears. We cried and someone paid attention. Not so in adulthood. Most folks are too preoccupied with themselves to notice a friend's or family member's depression. Those of us not feeling OK tend to disguise our depression so as not to bother anyone.

My advice: Give hugs and get hugs every day. Talk to friends and family and take time, every day, to think about what makes you happy, not what makes you miserable.

Learn to decompress while on vacation

Well, here I am on vacation in Provincetown, getting what I consider to be a much-needed break from the daily to-do list.

There is one major glitch – and it's me. Trying to do nothing is more of a chore for me than doing something. I actually was much better at relaxing when I was younger. Yes, even I, the grand poobah of stress management, have trouble letting go.

How sweet it is to watch children preoccupied for endless hours, ambling around curiously, involved with bugs, rocks, twigs or blades of grass. They seem to understand how to expand time.

When does time begin to make us its slave?

My first recollection of the end of timelessness was the rules that began around it – You have ten minutes left before you have to go to bed; You're getting too old for that; Hurry up, you'll be late for school!

And so we begin to live moments, not by relishing them, but by fearing them. "What if I'm not done on time?" There's a reason they came up with the term "deadline". We try to keep up with all the expectations built up around how valuable our time is. But the value is not determined by how much pleasure we derive. It shifts dramatically from simply being in the moment, to doing everything we can with the moment. And if the doing isn't productive, we feel guilty and unrewarded.

What will happen if there is no productive outcome? Surely someone is watching and reporting our total lack of responsibility. What if I can't tell anybody that I'm exhausted from everything I did today? No wonder when we finally get to a place that supports not doing anything that we often feel anxious and disoriented. Many people report that while on vacation, they need a couple of days just to unwind. By the time they come home they often look and feel more alive. Yet within a couple of weeks of racing the clock, they once again begin to look like castoffs of themselves.

The irony is that we all know that this mindset is crazy. Yet, like the rat that gets caught in the maze, we too get trapped in our perceptions of how to manage our time. I wonder how we would feel if we could add the concept of vacationing to our daily existence.

Could we make our lives a little more playful? Could we give ourselves permission to daydream? Can we integrate feelings of pleasure into the everyday? It doesn't have to be extraordinary, just taking ten minutes to lick an ice cream cone can feel delicious. We all need to smell the roses, because once those petals drop, there's nothing left but thorns, and we've all had enough of those.

Perfection isn't always the perfect goal to seek

Yesterday was Easter and I'm sure many families celebrated by attending religious ceremonies, followed by a great meal.

The children got the traditional baskets filled with chocolate bunnies and multicolored jelly beans. I somehow doubt that the traditional leather shoes and straw bonnets are still in the mix, which is rather sad for me. That has always been one of my fondest memories around the expectation of Easter.

The ritual of getting the outfit, hat and the shiny black leather shoes was such an exciting adventure. I couldn't wait to wear them, and when I did, I was extremely vigilant about protecting them from scuffs and scratches. I put Vaseline on them so they wouldn't crack. I would walk ever so carefully, trying to avoid any possibility of making my shoes look as though they were ever worn.

I often wonder if that wasn't one of the first clues that I was destined to be a perfectionist. When a scratch ultimately appeared, I would drive myself crazy trying to figure out where it came from and how it could have happened, since I had been so careful.

Some things never change; they just segue into different situations. My worry over keeping my shoes perfect turned into the need to keep my home looking as if it had never been lived in.

As a young mother of three, I often drove myself and everyone else crazy trying to keep the furniture upholstery looking new, the bathrooms scrubbed, the kitchen sink empty of any dishes and the rug with the nap running in the right direction.

I would often act like the inspector general, spending precious moments of my life maintaining things that would probably outlive me. Instead of enjoying the rewards of being in a comfortable, beautiful atmosphere and delighting in it with my family, I chose to tend to the needs of inanimate objects.

The sofa was never going to give me a hug, nor was the sink going to extol the virtues of being empty. I realize now that my focus was based on not realizing how irrational my drive to be perfect was. Once I became aware of how little joy there was in my endeavors, I started to become more aware of how to delight in what I had instead of trying to preserve it.

This does not mean that we take things for granted or abuse what we have. It's about striking a balance.

I do know one thing for sure – If I ever buy another pair of leather shoes, I will celebrate the scuffs with the full knowledge that they are on the feet of a woman who is more interested in going somewhere and doing something with her life than watching a pair of shoes stay new and unused.

We spend too much of our lives on hold nowadays

This morning I had to call a few places to make reservations for airline tickets, a hotel and, hopefully, a massage while I was at the hotel. My first holding pattern began, ironically, with the airlines. Being put on hold is not unfamiliar, but the latest and greatest way to keep a customer on hold is something new.

Companies used to play music that reminded one of the old elevator days. Over and over the tune continued until you thought: "Please, please, take it off." Then some fiend from Hell who was brought in to make sure that every moment of every day was cost-productive came up with a new and more insidious way to drive customers' nuts. They start the process by telling you that you could have gotten your information quicker if you simply went on the Internet and what an amazingly efficient way that is for you to get satisfaction. The only problem with that is that the website is not able to answer questions that haven't been programmed into it already.

Then the voice, which we know is not a real person, continues the message. Every program, perk and penalty is described, over and over and over. If you try to get out of the cycle, they ask you what you want and then give you the menu again. I dealt with this for at least twenty minutes, and then decided to go back to it after I tried to book the hotel. Unfortunately, the forces behind the airline's tortuous booking system had taken the hotel hostage and had made them part of the program. I was told the reservations agent was busy and then I got a complete rundown of every hotel property they had and where, the name of the restaurants in the hotels, the activities available and the rates. I was waiting for the names of the hotel personnel, how many pets they owned and whether they were married. They even went as far as to mention the thread count of the sheets.

At this point, I was ready to surrender, perhaps drive to Chicago and sleep on a park bench. My only fear was that a park ranger would be standing at the entrance asking me if I wanted to sleep on a bench made out of elm or oak and would I like it shaded or in the sun.

My last call was to the spa. When I heard that the receptionist was busy but that I could access the spa menu, I started to sweat. There were more than thirty choices and each one was either enlightened, innovative, calming, energizing or restoring. I wasn't sure how I was going to feel when I got there. Would I want to be restored but also calm? Or perhaps I needed to be energized and enlightened. I decided after two hours of trying to get what I needed that I didn't need anything.

Perhaps that's the real message. Too much of a good thing is just too much!

Lifestyle here and lifestyle there are different

I just returned from a trip to the south of France with my daughter and a good friend and I had a wonderful time. Not only did I get to rest and bask in the beauty, but I got to eat the most wonderful array of foods, especially bread.

Not a day or a meal went by that did not include bread. Crunchy, fresh and hot, served with olive oil. We would sit waiting with anticipation for the waiter to bring the basket heaped to the brim with its contents giving off an exquisite aroma. As we dipped and ate our bread, we would often comment that we really didn't need anything else, but then how could we leave out the pasta or salade niçoise that so often tempted us?

I know I'm beginning to sound like a nutcase, but I truly was struck with the fact that no one rushed her meal nor did anyone demonize bread, cheese or any other food as we do here. In fact, I never saw anyone walking around with food and eating it on the go. Now, it may be different in the more cosmopolitan areas such as Paris, but in the coastal areas it was as if I had gone back in time. There were many cafés where people sat and had their coffee and just people-watched. I saw no laptops as companions, or cell phones attached to ears. I'm sure those things exist there, but they are not part and parcel of everyday life.

Another thing that struck me was that the shops were closed on Sundays. It didn't matter how desperate you were, you had to wait until Monday. I had not been to Europe in quite some time, so the contrast in lifestyle was quite amazing to me. I love my country and all it has to offer, but I do believe we have lost our way when it comes to living life in balance. Not everyone has fallen prey to the persistent need to be busy every second, but the great majority of Americans are frantically running around, cell phone to the ear, trying to get things done. I think I have heard the following statement thousands of time from all walks of life: "I have so much to do!"

How and when did we trade our essential needs as human beings to become human doings? Why do the stores have to be open every day, some 24 hours a day? Why is it that not a day goes by where some food source has not become the new enemy? Carbohydrates, like pasta, were virtually ousted from our collective diet as if they were the archenemy of the human body. I saw very few heavy people on my trip, and spaghetti is a big staple of the diet in the Mediterranean.

Why don't we value taking time to eat and savor with family, friends or co-workers? Isn't the ability to connect with each other face to face more important than being on the lookout to see who e-mailed? Where is the value in being so preoccupied with all the gadgets and to-do lists rather than understanding that our lives are precious and that savoring them takes precedence over running around as if we were gerbils in a cage?

I hope that I can retain some of the feelings and insights I got from my trip. I brought home two gallons of olive oil to remind me to have my bread-and-dipping ritual with my meals. But beyond that, I hope to make a more conscious effort not to get caught up in doing, doing, doing and instead try to just *be*.

Losing stuff can prompt irrational questions and answers

I would love to do a study on how many hours we spend looking for things that we lose in our homes. I'm beginning to think it's at least half of our lives. Not a day goes by without me looking for my glasses. It used to be my car keys, too, but somehow I became vigilant about simply leaving them in the car. Suddenly, they are always there! The glasses are another issue. I use reading glasses and sometimes I also need distance glasses. The last time I got a new prescription I thought I would resolve the problem by buying a couple of pairs of each. I couldn't conceive of misplacing all of them. But, hey, what do I know? On any given day – you guessed it – they all disappear. They seem to have a life of their own.

Sometimes they are in the bathroom, sometimes the kitchen. What I really don't get is when I find them on top of the washer or dryer or next to the tub. The other day, after an hour of wild histrionics, I discovered them sitting outside on the front steps. But when it gets really scary is when you're looking for them and you realize you have them on.

I'm beginning to wonder if I'm on my way to memory slippage or if the glasses have taken on a life of their own and am a part of an alien society invested in taking over my mind. I watched "The Twilight Zone" years ago, and I think Rod Serling was onto something.

It's the craziness behind misplacing things that really gets to me. We become walking sitcoms asking anyone around us the most insane questions. I remember one day, back when I was married, looking for a shoe I couldn't find. I was in a hurry, and I scoured the entire house. Then I became totally irrational and accused my ex of taking it.

What would a six-foot man want with one size seven black pump? But, that kind of rationale doesn't even resonate with us when we're in that state of mind.

I think the question we ask the most is whether the person we live with has seen what we're looking for. Their response is always the same: "Well, where did you put it?" The answer is as nuts as the question. If I knew where I put it, I wouldn't be looking for it.

Shouldn't someone be inventing a tracking device that finds our stuff? I think it would make millions. I would also like them to invent something that helps us lose some things we really don't want to keep and are afraid to get rid of.

Well, if you have any ideas, let me know soon. I'm down to one pair of glasses and as of last night, they were missing in action.

Cat crazy:
Sometimes we act nuttier than our pets do

I've decided that if I ever get the opportunity to come back in another life, it's going to be as my cat.

He has the proverbial "Life of Riley". I know a lot of that has to do with the fact that he lives with someone who's crazy about him. He also came into my life when my need to be a control freak became much less of an issue.

I think if he had been part of my household when I was younger, he probably would have had to go into feline therapy. I never would have allowed him to jump up and sit on just about anything. I would have gone berserk if my duvet cover had hairs on it. I probably would have gotten a magnifying glass and picked them off one by one.

Certainly I never would have watched him lying around, staring, for no reason at all. How could that have been possible? After all, you need to be doing something so you're productive. Cats are definitely not productive. They just don't care.

My sleep being interrupted at strange hours would have gotten a lot of angry looks and loud sighs. Cats love to run around for no reason and seem to have discussions with other cats in the middle of the night.

In other words, they follow their bliss. They have a devil-may-care attitude about their masters. No matter what you do for them, they will not come when called or give affection unless it's their idea.

Cats are like heads of state. If they choose to receive you, they will; if not, you just have to wait. I have often watched my cat prance into my bedroom, head held high, tail straight up, with what looks like a smirk on his face. I begin begging him to come and cuddle with me, but he just looks at me blankly, knowing I will become even more pathetic in the next few minutes. I finally give up and ignore him. Then, and only then, does he decide to honor me with his presence. If only I had realized how seductive this type of behavior could be, I would have emulated it as a young woman. Who knows, I might have had dozens of men falling at my feet!

As for their food, it has to really excite them or they will just turn up their noses and walk off. I find myself asking him which can of Fancy Feast he wants. Then I give myself a dope slap and remind myself that I'm acting like a waiter and I'm talking to a cat. What will he do, pick up the phone and make a reservation at a local restaurant?

Maybe I should get a menu board and put it in the kitchen so I can go over it during the day. When I cooked for my kids, they ate what I cooked and that was that.

I have turned into a total nut bag. But I must admit that I would not have it any other way. This precious creature has brought me incredible joy and provided me with increased awareness on how and what should be done to protect all our animal friends.

Read a book:
The experience is like making a new friend

I've read more than once that reading is on the decline. I find that to be incredibly sad. This does not only pertain to books, but to newspapers and magazines as well. Bookstores used to be part of every downtown area.

Some still exist and thank goodness, for they are truly jewels that should be treasured. Unfortunately, many of the independent bookstores have been lost to the big chains, which were supposed to be bigger, better and could offer more discounted books.

The bigger stores also have cafés where you can grab a cup of coffee and a snack while you sink into one of the overstuffed chairs randomly placed around the store.

The concept proliferated, and soon we could find these retail giants across the country, but even they have not been able to keep up with the decline in reading.

One particular chain has been steadily losing profits and will soon be gobbled up by its competitor. My concern is not with profits but what we are losing and will lose by not honoring the act of reading the printed page.

Neuroscientists have shown that the brain needs exercise. Vocabulary is increased from reading. We not only see the words, but we see how to use them in a sentence.

Yes, you can read on the Internet, but the experience is simply not the same. It is meant to enable the "hurry sickness," which is so much a part of our stressed-out culture.

When we are reading from a book, we tend to linger, to reflect on what the author might have meant, to daydream and use our imaginations as if we were part of the plot.

One of my fondest memories as a child was being allowed to walk to the library, where I spent many hours wandering the aisles and then choosing the three books I was allowed to take out.

It was never an easy decision, but then I knew I could come back and choose again. Books have gotten me through many trials and tribulations.

They have provided me with amusement, greater understanding of the human condition, and amazing learning experiences. They have been my friends in good and bad times.

I encourage you and your family to take some time this summer to sit in a favorite spot and read. Turn off the cell phone, tell everyone to bug off, and go on an adventure that will enrich your mind and soul.

Stress management

I have taught stress management for almost thirty years. During that time, I have heard stories that cover almost every facet of human behavior. Some people can go through enormous trials and tribulations with grace and dignity, while others cannot deal with a hangnail without going nuts.

It used to be easier to be at ease, but today the media thrives on making us bonkers over every little thing. Not a week goes by without some report that someone or something is out to get us.

Gas prices escalating by leaps and bounds, foreclosures, banks going under, stocks and bonds tanking, airlines charging for suitcases and on and on.

There was a recent tomato scare that went on for weeks, but those tomatoes were given absolution and jalapenos took their place. Salmonella has become the scourge of the 21st century.

What makes some people able to go with the flow while others get frantic? I know part of the reason is biology. Some of us have brains that are over-reactive. We're like a tracking station, picking up life's debris at every turn.

Can we get better at navigating the ups and downs that can come our way no matter how much we think we're in control? Absolutely! But it takes effort to change a lifetime of automatic responses. Most of us don't even realize that much of how we live our lives is by being on autopilot. How often do you find yourself repeating statements you would love to just ditch or repeating unwanted behaviors you thought you had ditched?

Sometimes I think I've rented space in my head to an obnoxious roommate who wants to make my life miserable. Then I realize that it's my alter-ego trying to sabotage my happiness. It may sound crazy, but we all have inner critical voices that can make life a living hell.

So what can we do right here and now to begin to make our lives happier, more productive and less stressed? Here are my ten top suggestions:

- Think about what you're thinking about. Not everything you think makes sense is logical or sane.
- Ask yourself some of the questions you ask other people. You probably have the answer you're looking for.
- Keep moving. The more physical energy you use, the more relaxed you will be.
- Be a good listener. Talking without listening only allows you to have a one-sided conversation.
- Create generosity in your life. A generous person has an open heart.
- Say "Thank you" often. It really is one of the best gifts you can give another person.
- Read every day and make sure you learn something new. It will help you to not get boring and repetitive.
- Do something for someone else that will enhance their life. It will make yours better, too.
- Honor the elderly with visits and compassion. You will get there, too (maybe).
- S.M.I.L.E. (**S**ee **M**iracles **I**n **L**ife **E**very Day). It will keep you from getting jaded and cynical.

Dressing for a wedding

I'm getting ready to go to a wedding this weekend and I started thinking of weddings I've attended in the past.

I keep going over what I'm going to wear and whether I will be too hot or cold in it. What shoes should I choose? High heels to make me look longer, leaner and more contemporary, but will end up killing my feet after the first hour. Or maybe I should select something comfy and cozy that will make me look like I borrowed it from my grandmother?

The outfit I originally chose has a top that needs a strapless bra. I just realized I don't have one. So now, I have to go shopping the night before I leave to find the right undergarment. I could choose another outfit, which I just might do.

It's hard to feel comfortable at an afternoon wedding when it's hot and humid.

When I was younger, I only cared about making a statement. So what if the shoes that have criss-cross straps bore a hole into your flesh and forced you to take an antibiotic to stop a massive infection?

Who cares if your dress is so tight that you have to wear a "girdle" to flatten everything so you don't look like a sausage with legs? It's the "wow" comments that you're looking for. You might not be able to eat or drink all day and night so the outfit doesn't explode on your body, but what the heck; it's worth it, right?

And let's not forget hauling a handbag full of makeup and breath mints so that your breath smells fresh and your lipstick is perfect at all times. After all, you're going to be in some wedding photos, and who wants to look like they live in Appalachia?

Well, the times they are a-changing, and I'm choosing to feel loose and cool. Age has its benefits, and one of them is you realize that you don't have to torture yourself.

I know now that feet swell and they need room, so I guess I'm going for the shoes that can slip on and off with great ease.

I may wear a shift dress, which has room for growth as the evening wears on. I might even take a sleeping bag and take a snooze under the table. Now there's an idea. It might be bigger than a "Snuggie".

Just when you can't stand one more boring conversation from a distant relative, you excuse yourself and take a nap.

Shut-eye craver

Nothing beats a good night's sleep. Not only do you wake up refreshed, you've also got energy to spare.

I never had sleep issues as a teen. I always slept through the night but could often snooze away the day. It felt like I was in "The Twilight Zone". Despite my mother, hands on hips, barking out orders to "get up" and "get moving," my body and mind were somehow unable to connect. I eventually came out of my stupor, but it literally took a couple of hours to shake it off.

Those days are long gone. Children, worries, a husband who snored, extensive travel with lots of time changes, and, finally, menopause have all changed my sleep patterns.

I sleep, but not in the same way. I fall asleep but seem to wake up at 2:30 a.m. on a regular basis. I've thought about joining a neighborhood watch group so I could use the time productively, but who wants to get up and get dressed at that hour?

Maybe my body still thinks I have to do a nighttime feeding. I eventually fall back to sleep, but not without some time spent going over stuff that should have been buried with one of the pharaohs – old wounds, unfulfilled dreams, injustices, blah, blah, blah.

The mind is often like a bunch of monkeys looking for bananas. I have used the methods I teach others to quell the mental cacophony, but it doesn't always work.

It's especially hard now because of a frog that has made my fish pond his summer residence. He seems to love to sound off every fifteen minutes like a fog horn alerting incoming ships. This is a loud frog. A friend of mine heard him while we were talking on the phone.

I decided to see if I could find him amid all the flora and fauna in the pond. It didn't take long, because he was splayed on a lily pad as bold as could be. He didn't flinch as I came closer to observe. He started his braying when I got near. I laughed.

Maybe if I get close enough I can kiss him, and he'll turn into a prince and take me away to a beautiful castle where I'll get a good night's sleep.

Don't beat yourself up with what-ifs

Whenever I do a seminar on stress management, I always get a majority of individuals who want to discuss the past and how different their lives would have been if they had made better decisions.

It's all well and good to visit the past if it serves as a way to learn valuable lessons that make life more meaningful. Unfortunately, most people act as if they are prisoners of their pasts. Albert Ellis, a renowned expert in the field of cognitive behavioral therapy, coined a phrase I absolutely love. He calls getting stuck in what-ifs – "should-ing on yourself".

I should have gotten a different job. I should have married someone else. I should exercise more, eat better, and on and on. If you can relax and stop "should-ing on yourself," you're going to enjoy life much more.

Here are some steps to help you live more in the here and now:
- Whenever you get caught up in thinking about what you should have done, stop and think about what a waste of energy that is. You can't go back and redo it, because that period of time has passed. As long as you're still breathing, there's a possibility that you can do it now.

However, if you have no intention to follow through, give it up and move on.
- Buy yourself a whip and keep it handy. Every time you start to drown yourself or others in "shoulds," grab the whip and give yourself a good beating. You're already self-flagellating, so why not literally do it?
- Keep a "should" journal. You'll probably be shocked to discover how many times a day "shoulda, coulda, woulda" comes out of your mouth.

There are certain things that have to be done in life. Do them to the best of your ability and then forget about them.

Don't allow "should-ing" to go on at home or at work. Ask people to express themselves in better ways. "Should-ing" is filled with judging and finding fault. As a result, our surroundings become a courtroom filled with prosecutors and attorneys. Life is too precious to waste on what might have been. Get over it, get on with it and live "now".

Overkill: Why can't we just leave well enough alone?

About fifteen years ago I took my first trip to Seattle. As I got off the plane I was struck by the amazing aroma of coffee that seemed to permeate the airport. It was so seductive that I had to find the source and experience it.

It turned out to be Starbucks. The setting was reminiscent of a European café with soft jazz in the background. The choices were simple because there were just several blends.

The hook was you could hang out and drink it with friends or solo while reading or simply watching other people.

As I ambled through the city I discovered a few more Starbucks. I asked if they were anywhere else in the States and they said not yet, but it was being considered.

Well, expand they did. They're everywhere.

Doesn't it feel that Americans love to take something that starts out being a great idea to the place where the original premise gets lost because of overkill?

I recently read that Starbucks is now downsizing and removing the extras they created to go with their coffees because they're losing money. DUH!

The smell of food fights the smell of coffee.

Dunkin' Donuts just announced that they're adding more food. Why can't we leave "well enough" alone?

I really don't need to get a pizza in a coffee bar or a steak with fries at the dry cleaners. There are places that already do that.

Maybe Victoria's Secret should start selling oysters on the half shell with their thongs. They are considered an aphrodisiac, so that might make sense.

Maybe the real way to make a profit is to stick to what you know best.

But that takes common sense.

An evolved species

Over the years I have turned my backyard into a sumptuous garden. I love flowers, shrubs and plants of all kinds and the critters they attract.

On any given day my yard is visited by hummingbirds, cardinals, finches, an occasional woodpecker, bees and butterflies. I often see chipmunks scurrying about, and I know there's a skunk somewhere because every once in a while he lets loose with a fragrance with which we are all familiar.

It all comes together in a most delightful way with one exception.

The squirrels.

Oh, don't get me wrong, I love squirrels. In fact, I'm beginning to believe they are an evolved species that are far superior to us.

Several years ago, I innocently put up a bird feeder, hanging it from one of the trees. It attracted a variety of birds, but within a day I watched in horror as one squirrel, then several, gulped down the feed in what seemed like minutes.

I periodically ran out flailing my arms wildly and shouting profanities. They would disappear for a few minutes and, just as I deluded myself that I had somehow diverted them from their appointed task, they reappeared.

Over and over, I ran outside like someone possessed, periodically repeating my former tirades. Friends shared their squirrel stories, and one told me to get a cone to put over the feeder – which, they assured me, would be impossible for them to stay on. I have since realized that the word "impossible" is not in a squirrel's vocabulary.

So I, the eternal optimist, got the cone and watched as the critters tumbled off, one after another. I felt such delight that I had outwitted them.

But squirrels, aside from being clever, have definitely trained with the Cirque du Soleil troupe, and have done extensive graduate work at M.I.T. One of their foremost squirrel engineers figured out how you could balance on the apex of the cone and grab the seed. He then sent one of their top gymnasts to try out his formula, and voila, success.

The others followed his lead, and in minutes the seed was gone.

The conclusion I've now reached is that we need to get squirrels into public institutions, especially government. I am convinced that they would create solutions quickly and efficiently, and be able to save us a lot of money.

Enjoy life:
Confessions of a former perfectionist

When I was younger, I was such a perfectionist! Everything had to be done by me personally. Everything I cooked was done from scratch. I used to clean everything, sew, knit, paint walls, dress my kids perfectly and try to look like a fashion plate every day.

People would come to my house and say, "Oh, I love your drapes!" and I'd say, "I made them myself!"

"I smell bread!"

"Baked it myself," I'd answer.

"Are those your children?"

"Yeah, I made 'em myself!"

I think of the silly things I said back then, such as, "You could eat off my floors."

Now, isn't that special? Imagine having people over and having them eat off your floors.

I was also a slave to rules. I did things and didn't even know why I was doing them. One day, I was cooking a roast and I cut the ends off and threw them away, as I always did. It occurred to me to wonder why, so I called my mother.

"Why do we cut the ends off?" I asked.

"I don't know why you're doing it," she answered. "I did it because it didn't fit in the pan."

After thirty or more years of mopping, scouring, dusting and checking to see that everything is right, I'm seriously considering throwing in the towel (if you'll excuse the expression). Life is not just a daily list of to-dos. It also needs a serious sprinkling of ta-dahs. So here are some suggestions for those of you who feel compelled to work yourself into a dither about everything and have to have everything and everyone around you perfect:

- Make a "not-to-do" list. Write down everything you've done already or what you have enough of. For example, "Have plenty of toilet paper, soap, and remembered my mother's birthday."
- Make your bed but leave one side undone. As you leave the room, remind yourself that the bed checkers are not coming.
- Tell one person one thing that you don't do well. Maybe the underwear and socks in your drawers are not lined up perfectly.
- Go outside when it's raining and get all wet. Try it sometime when you have something good on.
- Let someone borrow your good pencil or pen when you're at work, and let the family use the good towels. After all, they are your loved ones.

But most of all, don't forget to enjoy your life. That's the greatest ta-dah of all!

Chapter 2

Health, Healing and Happiness

"The body heals with play, the mind heals with laughter, and the spirit heals with joy."

~Proverb

Why do some studies point out the obvious?

There isn't a day that goes by that I am not exceedingly amused by our society's need to prove the obvious. I call it the "big duh"!

A recent newspaper article headlined the following: Grief Affects Health. It appears that the surviving spouse from an unhappy marriage is likely to have fewer, less expensive health problems than a spouse who loses a partner from a happy marriage, according to a new study by Yale researchers. The article went on to say that "Sigmund Freud found that ambivalent and conflicted relationships would predispose the survivor to pathological grief," however, the latest research shows that losing a partner in a harmonious marriage puts you at greater risk for health problems. Have any of these scientists watched a film called "The Perfect Murder", read the latest newspaper headlines, or scanned the police blotters, which are riddled with cases of domestic violence?

I doubt sincerely whether these people were playing kissy face with each other while smacking each other around. Unless of course it was part of some real kinky lifestyle. Isn't it apparent that if you and your mate spend most of your waking moments feeling upset, irritated, and angry with each other, you're going to experience a high degree of stress?

Have you ever heard anyone say during the course of a conversation that they couldn't wait to go home so they could get pissed off at their significant other? Hello! That's why we have something called divorce.

After an extended period of not getting along, you usually call a lawyer. If that person dies before you go to court, you may or may not experience some sadness. However, although we might hate to admit it, there's probably a sigh of relief. Your stress level comes down and you're free.

If you're absolutely crazy about someone who passes away, the sadness will engulf you and it will cause you a great deal of physical and mental problems. Grief debilitates the immune system. There are studies that show that many individuals will come down with a major illness after the death of a loved one.

It stands to reason that if we are mind/body/spirit, then our bodies will leap along with our minds. When we lose a loved one, we have lost a part of ourselves. In essence, the "us" is gone and we are left with the "I". When my grandfather died, my grandmother's sadness filled every corner of the house. They lived with my family when I was a child, and I will never forget how his passing affected me.

It does not take a rocket scientist to figure any of this out, but I'm sure we'll soon be reading about another study that has discovered that people who starve themselves die. Duh!

Life is full of additives

Has anyone out there noticed that you can't buy anything anymore that does not have added ingredients? I'm not talking about obvious additives like yeast so the bread will rise or nuts that will make it crunchy. I'm talking about a marriage between herbs or vitamins, and anything they come in contact with.

There are tortilla chips that have Saint John's Wort in them. Is that in case you get depressed if you eat the whole bag?

I saw a shampoo the other day that had Ginkgo Bilbao in it – an herbal memory aid. Do you really care if you remember that you washed your hair? Or is it supposed to seep into your brain while you wash?

I recently got a cold and thought I might try some zinc tablets, since there has been some interesting research showing it can shorten the duration of a cold. Every package I looked at contained Vitamin C, Echinacea, calcium, and whatever is considered the healing model of the moment.

Are we a nation of hypochondriacs? Or are we a bunch of lemmings driven by Madison Avenue's latest assault on our intelligence? It appears that the way to hook us is to sell us on something that's supposed to be good for us. If vitamin C is good, then let's put it in everything. I wouldn't be surprised to find it in laundry soap. Clean clothes that don't look sick!

Ginkgo is the newest obsession. It's supposed to help your memory. Although the latest study found that there was very little correlation, it's still popping up in everything. When I went to school, we had to remember long stanzas of poetry and recite it in front of the classroom. In fact, memorization was a very big part of my educational process.

So here's another big duh: when you force your brain to remember, it creates new pathways so it can create more memory. However, it takes work to memorize anything, and by and large we are a pill-popping, remote control society. If it takes too long, we don't want to do it. Unless of course it has commercial value.

If we all were told that our cholesterol was going to go down and our net worth would go up if we learn to memorize the complete works of Carl Sandburg, we just might do it.

In the meantime, take note of how much of these supplements are in the various foods you're ingesting. There *is* something called too much of a good thing.

Start by using your common sense. What a novel idea! Do you eat a balanced diet? How's your energy level? Nature has provided us with a wonderful array of foods.

Check in with a dietician and find out if you're eating well. He or she may recommend a multiple vitamin or they may not. In the meantime, become a smart consumer. What's hot today is not hot tomorrow. You may actually feel better and live longer if you read more poetry.

Reading is the cure-all for boredom

I am, quite frankly, obsessed with books. So when I was asked to do a fundraiser for the Plymouth Public Library, I said yes.

Everyone who is near and dear to me knows that I cannot be left alone for any length of time in a bookstore. The result is often a pile so high that it takes a Sherpa to carry them to the car.

I can thank my mother for my interest in reading. There was no chance for boredom in my house. A claim of "I'm bored" automatically got the response, "Go read a book."

One of my earliest birthday presents was a library card. Saturday was my big outing to the library. I felt so important when the librarian asked me for my card.

My mother constantly pushed education and culture. I never heard her tell me I was cute or beautiful, which might have been a nice touch, but I did hear, "Beauty fades, but you always have your brains."

Now, of course, we know you can lose both your beauty and your brains. Although with the advancements of plastic surgery you have a good chance of reversing a sagging chin. It's easier to retain a youthful brain though; all you need to do is read. It's less painful, too.

Exciting new brain research shows that aging does not necessarily atrophy the thinking process. Rather, it is about the lack of new input that makes the brain less agile.

Unfortunately, over the last twenty years or so,

as a culture we have become less interested in reading.

We have become a nation of watchers — television watchers. Flip on the TV and become a mindless blob. Oh, sure, there are interesting and provocative shows that could get us to think. But not like the written word, which encourages the brain to continue to use its ability to learn vocabulary.

Without this constant refresher course in language, both old and new, the brain begins to lose its ability to allow us to have conversations with each other in ways that are exciting and interesting.

If we continue on this course of non-reading, we will soon be communicating through a system of grunts.

Don't let a lack of time be an excuse for not reading. Keep a book with you at all times. We never know when we will have the opportunity to read a few pages. It beats getting upset while you're waiting for someone, and it's far superior to most of the so-called entertainment they have on television. The most exciting part of reading is that it gives us the ability to think, explore and experience a most wondrous human talent: the written word.

Life used to be much easier than it is now

My mother, who has an incredible ability to observe the ridiculous, commented on the fact that nobody seems to be able to do anything anymore without someone telling them how to do it.

She mentioned that since everyone is getting so entrenched in what experts think, pretty soon they won't be able to leave the house without asking someone's advice. She figured she'd make millions by writing a book called "Leave, Then Come Back".

Of course, she also managed to point out that people hired me to learn how to laugh at their stress – something that her family did every day, along with consuming spaghetti and wine. It appears that there is absolutely nothing a human being does today that doesn't have a self-help book attached to it.

If you're talking to someone, it is no longer just a conversation. If it's a man, we can't talk the way a woman does because he hears things differently. If you don't say it the right way, he might get mad and leave town.

My grandparents didn't give a hoot about who got mad. They just yelled back and forth at each other.

My grandfather would shout: "Fatti, i fatti tuoi! (Mind your own business!)" My grandmother would respond with "Sei pazzo! (You're crazy!)" Suddenly the whole thing would end just as quickly as it started and they would start discussing what they wanted to eat for dinner. They were married for more than fifty years without ever reading a book on relationships.

Yes, I do believe in progress. We know a lot more about how to communicate and what could make a marriage better. But the divorce rate is higher than ever.

You used to be able to take a walk whenever you felt like it without much concern for how fast or slow you were going or what kind of footwear you had on. Now, you have to strap on a pedometer, wear the right clothing and footwear, carry a water bottle, and don't forget your cell phone in case you have a heart attack.

Meanwhile, you no longer look like someone who's out to enjoy a pleasant outing but rather like a member of a SWAT team. Nothing feels simple anymore. If it does, you're almost certain that you're not doing whatever it is the right way.

So much of life is about common sense. It is a quality that is part of a natural radar screen. It allows us to sort out what is valuable from what is ridiculous. If we lose it, we will be condemned to needing a training manual to sort out the trash.

Or perhaps the dog, who can still think on his own, will be taking us for a walk.

Men vs. women: Loyalty bridges the differences (All of the books and research can't take the place of mutual devotion)

I often wonder how my grandmother and grandfather stayed together for almost sixty years before one of them passed away. I remember them yelling at each other periodically, but neither one of them ever packed their bags and moved out.

My grandfather was able to stand my grandmother's pouting and posturing by absorbing himself in reading his daily Italian newspaper while savoring his espresso.

If he didn't look up, she would add audible sighing, which often sounded like a cow giving birth.

If he started to show signs of irritation, she knew enough to "cool it" and would start talking about what they were going to cook that night. Food was definitely their common ground.

I loved watching how animated they would become as they whipped together their magical ingredients that became dishes that would make family and friends beg for more.

There were no books to read about how different men and women are, nor were there relationship coaches or therapists to help them understand each other. Male and female brains and their differences were not even a consideration. Earlier scientists might have been able to investigate these differences only by studying the brains of cadavers, but thanks to advances in genetics and non-invasive brain-imaging technology, we are now able to see inside the brain in real time.

John Gray was one of the first authors to ride the wave of male/female differences. His book *Men Are from Mars, Women Are from Venus* sold millions of copies. One of his observations was that men like to be alone with their thoughts while women like to be in concert with other women and talk about just about anything.

MRI scans can back this up by showing that the brain circuitry for language and the ability to observe emotions is more prevalent in women.

Many books today have made us realize that men usually don't like to walk around stores with us, notice that the sofa has been moved, or be disturbed when they're in the middle of a football game.

I don't know if my grandparents realized any of that, but they did know that loyalty to each other was tantamount to a long-lasting relationship, and I don't think you'll find that in a book or a brain scan.

Go with the flow

Every day, I get "Google alerts" about happiness – How to get happy, what makes you happy, or how to stay happy.

I signed up for these alerts because I have been invested in teaching positive psychology for several years, but I've started thinking about how daunting it is to try to be happy. All of the articles and books are starting to make me feel like being happy is a job.

There are now huge bodies of research on happiness. Happy people are grateful, loving, kind, generous, accountable, responsible, civil and more. My grandmother never even went to high school, but she seemed to know that the above values worked. She actually demanded them of her family, but she never added, "You'll be happy if you do them."

I love that we can now identify certain behaviors and see how they affect our minds and bodies, but sometimes I want to scream, "Enough already!"

There are a lot of things that make me and a lot of other people happy that might just fall into the category of being ordinary, and will never become research projects.

I personally like staring into space, eating an ice cream cone, especially when it gets down to the itty, bitty bottom. I love acting silly, talking to my cat and eating a plate of spaghetti loaded with parmesan cheese.

I adore all my magazines, books, watching *Dancing With the Stars* and *So You Think You Can Dance*.

I have had many thrills imagining myself leaping through the air.

I'm thrilled that my three children and eleven grandchildren have never done anything that required doing time or being part of a reality show.

"My slippers rock!" What could be more exciting than having your foot enveloped in fur on a cold morning?

Being able to hook my bra myself and being able to fit in my clothes day to day is really exciting.

I really feel happy when I manage to keep my house and yard picked up so that I'm not found in a heap of clutter in my final days.

But perhaps the thing that has really brought me the most happiness is that I've learned to be comfortable in my skin.

Happiness tips, no matter how many, won't do that for you. It is a daily process of learning to go with the flow and not being caught up in believing that you need a manual to "be happy".

Sometimes we are better off not knowing

Every morning I spend time reading the latest magazines and newspapers. I have done this for a majority of my life. Most of the articles written years ago focused on recipes, crafts, interior design and parenting. There were also some really funny pieces about the expectations around women written by the wonderfully gifted writer Erma Bombeck.

I loved reading Erma. She was so aware of the absurdities of life. Her talent to expose the ridiculous helped millions take themselves less seriously.

As I flipped through the pages of my current pile of periodicals, I realized that most of what I was reading made me feel that nothing is safe and that most of us need a lot of help.

Did you know that handrails, bank countertops, faucets on airplanes and restroom sinks are loaded with bacteria that could make you deathly sick? Now you do. Why should I be the only one aware that I may get a deadly plague as a result of touching something?

Here's the joke: We've been told to wash our hands often during cold season to avoid the sniffles. Now we have a real dilemma. We can take a chance and get a cold by not washing. Or wash and wait to see if we get something worse because we might have touched the faucet.

Mold allergies are another fear factor. Mold can take over your whole house. You could wake up one morning and find that you and your family have become a penicillin factory.

You need to also check your entire self for hidden sun damage. It's not enough to slather your exposed flesh with sunscreen. You now need to know that the parts of your body that are covered could also be in danger because of the type of clothing you have on. Certain fabrics are not as sun-resistant as others, so you need to slather your entire body before you get dressed.

One more thing to do.

Other things to be on the alert for are dry mouth, which can cause cavities, cats with sore throats, mites that infest pillows and sheets, salad bars, mad cow disease and monkey pox. This is only the tip of the iceberg.

And the only way to avoid it is to encase yourself in a plastic bubble – after you've put on your sunscreen, eaten foods that have been tested by NASA, and made sure that no one or anything ever comes in contact with you.

Ultimately, you just have to laugh at the whole thing.

My grandmother lived to be ninety-three. When a piece of food fell on the floor she brushed it off and ate it. Poor thing. She lived a long life totally uninformed.

Things we might know if we used some sense

I keep trying to understand why Americans find it so hard to have common sense. I always remember my grandparents and my mother being so aware of the obvious. We spend millions of dollars on researching and discussing what we know to be true before we allow ourselves to believe it. Not a day goes by without a news report or article giving us the results of yet another study.

Now, I love how adept we have become at understanding how our minds and bodies function and what can help or hinder them, but how far do we have to go to convince people of some simple truths? For example: If you use a smaller plate, you eat less. Now *that* takes at least an IQ of 200 to recognize.

Here's another one: People who are sleep-deprived have more accidents and poor memory quality. Really! Or: If you get angry a lot, you are more susceptible to strokes and heart attacks. Imagine that! How about: Laughing makes you feel good. Well, can you believe it? Until I read that, I thought I should go out and complain all night so I could wake up refreshed and happy.

The latest idiotic finding is that people who don't take time for scheduled meals eat more snacks and seem to lose sight of the difference between a snack and a meal. Lunch hour was part of what employees looked forward to. It gave them that necessary hour to refresh their bodies and souls by refueling themselves through food and conversation. Now, the majority of people either run errands during their lunch hour, work through it, or read or watch TV while they are supposed to be eating.

I've watched people eating while they're driving, holding the wheel with their knees while they stuff themselves. It is virtually impossible to satiate your hunger when you are racing to get somewhere while you're eating and also trying not to get killed. How can you even remember what you ate? You could be eating sawdust on rye and you probably wouldn't know it. What ends up happening is that you forget what and how much you ate because of being preoccupied with driving and probably talking on your cell phone. And so, before too long, you're looking to eat again.

This mindless eating segues into our home lives. I am often appalled at how many people have the TV on during dinner. It does not take much to realize that you will eat more when you are preoccupied. It is no wonder that there are so many people with gastric reflux. How can the body cooperate in digesting the fuel it needs when it is competing with your brain watching the news or any other program that may stress you?

When I was a child, I was allowed no distraction while eating. No phone calls, no radio, no TV. The only thing to do was savor the food, compliment Mama and have a good conversation. My grandparents and parents never read studies, they just tapped into a wisdom that seemed to know how the human spirit could thrive and survive. Maybe it's time we all tried the same thing.

Let's stop treating teens as if they're adults; they're not

In the last several years, a lot of research has come out about the teenage brain. Most recently, a new review suggests that billions of dollars have been wasted on education and intervention programs to dissuade teens from dangerous activities. Lo and behold, neuroscientists have discovered that teenagers have immature brains that are not yet capable of avoiding risky behaviors. The studies, spearheaded by Jay Giedd of the National Institute of Mental Health, have found that the brain is not fully developed until after age eighteen. In particular, the area of the brain that regulates impulse and emotions is underdeveloped in teenagers.

I imagine this information validates what millions of parents already know intuitively. Junior might hear you but that doesn't mean he "gets it". Unfortunately, we seem to be a culture that likes to assign maturity to people who really haven't lived long enough to earn it. I have witnessed over and over parents who start talking to their children as if the kids were adults when they are still in the high chair. They tell them something like, "Have some more vegetables" and then they go on about why they should as if the kid has the capability to understand the reasons. When the child grunts or goos, they perceive it as a response that they've understood.

Haven't you been in the presence of a couple who go on and on explaining things to their 3-, 4- or 5-year-old because the child keeps saying "no" to their requests? It boggles the mind.

When did we become so foolish? I don't remember having a lot of things explained to me. They were simply orders of the day, such as, "Wake up, you have to go to school", or "Clean your room", or "Mind your manners". It was not very complicated. My grandparents and my mother just didn't think that explaining was necessary.

Primitive tribes have understood the laws of ascension forever. Each period of a person's life had a ritual attached to it before progressing to the next step. They also had to listen to the advice of elders. Teenage boys and girls had many rituals and things they had to accomplish before they were considered adults. That didn't necessarily mean their brains were any more mature because they had to sleep in the forest for a week, but at least there was an understanding that the baton of maturity was not handed to a child without the permission of the community.

We come up with slogans like "Just say no" and have teens sign anti-drug pledges and think that those acts will somehow be absorbed into their brain structure. Some teens may have that ability, but it's time we all really understood that a lot of who we are is driven by our biology. If a child's or teen's brain does not have the neurological brakes to stop them from harming themselves or others, shouldn't we begin to make sure parents get this information either through the schools or the media? Wouldn't it be great to know that even though you told your 17-year-old son to drive carefully, or to not drink because he could end up in jail, that he really knew what that meant? It's important for parents to know that he might not.

Procrastination

Procrastination has been the subject of thousands of articles. I have read many of them in the hopes that I would learn how to reach deadlines without driving myself crazy.

My battle with procrastination goes back to childhood when I would hide under the covers studying furtively for a test the next day. My mother's pleas to do a little every day went in one ear and out the other. Nothing seemed to prevent me from waiting until the last minute, even though doing so elevated my stress level to "code blue".

It seems that some things never change. The ultimate irony is that I would lecture my children on the very same issue, giving them all the sound advice that I knew could make *my* life easier. I thought perhaps maturity would kick in and I would somehow segue into not "putting things off". Unfortunately, some things never do change.

I find myself still managing to do anything and everything other than the thing that has to be done. Most often it is about deadlines. The very word is off putting. Why put the word "dead" into it? It really feels like a funeral is imminent.

Shouldn't we have a word that makes us feel like we're joyful about accomplishing something? How about using the same rhetoric athletes use, like "the finish line". That feels euphoric and fun.

I think some people fare better doing things last minute. I feel I do far better when I don't take a lot of time. I realize that what I am revealing about myself flies in the face of rational thinking.

But I recently received a newsletter from Robert Biswas-Diener, a researcher in positive psychology, who shared some research that may actually authenticate my feelings. He and a colleague are discovering that many people process ideas subconsciously – or "incubate" – and then rise to the occasion at the last moment and complete their work.

They are conducting further research to find out more about the motivational factors that influence this type of behavior.

So you just might be an "incubator" – putting off important work, but often getting superior results. If so, you might want to let yourself off the hook. Just be realistic; certain projects and jobs do need more time. I wouldn't want to be in a plane with a pilot who waited to land until there was no more fuel. That's called stupid!

Training your brain

I recently read an article titled "How to Train the Aging Brain". I am fascinated with these types of articles because my brain is definitely aging and I want to do everything I can to prevent it from becoming older than it needs to be.

Jack Mezirow, professor emeritus at Columbia Teachers College, posits that adults learn best if presented with what he calls a "disorienting dilemma" or something that "helps you critically reflect on the assumptions you've acquired".

Easier said than done. How often do we dig our heels in and defend our positions about what we think?

I have found, over the years when I am teaching a workshop on stress management, that most people find it incredibly difficult to change their assumptions. Most of us like the comfort of our perspectives. Staying wrapped in a cocoon of thoughts that feels familiar helps us stay stuck in the status quo.

How many times have you heard someone say, "Don't rock the boat", "Don't make waves", or "Leave it alone"? Certainly all those phrases have merit when the occasion calls for it. But more often than not, we need to stop and listen to how we really feel about a situation rather than taking it at face value.

A friend of mine always takes me to task for going over and over how I handled certain situations. Her modus operandi is more devoted to standing in the wings and waiting for someone else to make the decision for her. She would never question her thinking process because she might have to do things differently.

Once we go down that path, a whole tsunami of issues might crop up. Individuals around you might start to think that you have a mind of your own and then they might have to question how they relate to you.

I spent a great deal of my younger years staying on the safe side. If I never questioned my assumptions, then I would never have to mature and grow.

My career choice threw me into models of thinking that have consistently challenged my thinking patterns.

Stop and listen occasionally to how and what you're thinking about. Become the witness to your thoughts; you may be surprised and delighted, or you may be horrified.

Either way, you may just discover that you have much more control over your mind than you ever imagined.

Sometimes it takes practice to be happy

Almost every magazine I pick up lately has an article in it on how to be happy. Unfortunately, happiness is somewhat contingent on our biology.

According to research by psychologists at the University of Minnesota and the University of Illinois, no matter what happens, people tend to return to a genetically fixed level of happiness.

David Tellegen and David Lykken at Minnesota found that twins share a "characteristic mood level," even when raised separately. Tellegen noted that even actor Christopher Reeve, left paralyzed after a horseback-riding accident, seemed to have regained his naturally optimistic outlook.

Yet, those who believe that heredity may be a basis for happiness also say that that doesn't mean a person can't change. But change as we all know is a very difficult process, especially for those of us who are invested in maintaining the status quo.

The familiar, even though it doesn't serve our best interests, is easier. Let's face it: if my favorite thing to do is have a gallon of ice cream every night, washed down with forty ounces of Coke, and I'm in ecstasy every time I do it, I doubt that I will want to trade that experience for a low-fat snack and a glass of carrot juice.

Most people need a life crisis or a high school reunion to make significant changes. However, there is hope if we take some time to examine our beliefs. I'm sure we've all heard this famous quote by the late Mary

Kay: "If you think you can, or you think you can't, you're right."

I have always been extremely frustrated by the fact that it is much easier to elicit thoughts and feelings that make us feel mentally and physically unhealthy. However, I do know that with practice, we can embrace a more optimistic outlook, and that in itself could lead to a happier, more fulfilling life.

The following poem by Portia Nelson expresses it best:

I walk down the street.
There is a deep hole in the sidewalk.
I fall in. I am lost. I am helpless. It isn't my fault.
It takes forever to find a way out.

I walk down the same street.
There is a deep hole in the sidewalk.
I pretend I don't see it. I fall in again.
I can't believe I am in this place, but it isn't my fault.
It still takes a long time to get out.

I walk down the same street.
There is a deep hole in the sidewalk.
I see it is there. I still fall in, it's a habit.
My eyes are open. I know where I am. It is my fault.
I get out immediately.

I walk down the same street.
There is a deep hole in the sidewalk.
I walk around it.

I walk down another street.

Share happiness with friends

A recent study of happiness conducted by Dr. David Lykken of the University of Minnesota seems to indicate that, for the most part, we human beings are each born with our own individual capacity for feeling happiness.

Whether we win the lottery or lose a spouse, chances are that our happiness "set point" will not vary all that much in the course of our lives.

The search for "happiness" through the attainment of something external – career success, wealth, beauty, consumer objects – now seems to have been proven by science to be pointless. It doesn't work.

I love this finding for many reasons, but probably most of all because it's almost exactly what my grandmother Francesca always said to us.

You won't find happiness by looking outside or by trying to attain wealth or status. You only find happiness at home. What does seem to make us happier are the little things: the smell of someone cooking your breakfast in the morning, the feeling of holding a child's hand, the majesty of a perfect sunset, the sharing of laughter. It's those things that make life worth living, and that can make us feel like a happier human being. The more we allow ourselves to enjoy those little things, the happier we become.

And the best way, always, to have wonderful moments is to share them with others. Think of people as if they were vitamin supplements! Because, in fact, that's just what they are.

Other people can help supplement our own natural internal resources: they can give us strength, they can give us clarity, they can help cure depression, and lower our blood pressure.

Instead of St. John's Wort, spend an hour with your friend, Ruby, who makes you laugh.

Instead of ginseng, which they say is good for vitality levels, spend half an hour at the park with your friend, Kevin the jock.

Instead of Hops, which they say is good for a lack of appetite, invite a few friends over, spend some time in the kitchen preparing a sumptuous and satisfying meal, and share an evening of community, friendship and food.

Fight the urge towards privacy – it's overrated! Privacy leads to isolation, and isolation leads to loneliness. Whenever we feel lonely, we tend to overeat, drink too much, and buy something we don't need, or focus on negative thoughts and problems. The only thing that truly satisfies that need is connections to friends and family.

Try it; you'll feel better. I guarantee it.

Chapter 3

Look Back, So You Can Look Forward

"Forget the past, but remember what it taught you."

~Anonymous

Life today presents too many choices

I think I've come up with a new job. It's called a choice assistant.

What do they do? Well, they help you decide things.

What things? I don't know about you, but I'm getting more confused with each passing day. Nothing is easy anymore.

If I go out to eat, they hand me a 30-page menu. It includes foods I've known about for the better part of my life, like steak, shrimp, pasta and fish, but now there are subcategories. There's petite filet, steak tips, rib eye, venison, ostrich and alligator. Pasta used to be linguine and angel hair. Now it's pappardelle, farfalle, rigatoni, tortellini, and who knows what else.

Fish can be tilapia, orange roughy, sturgeon, mahi mahi, and catfish. Doesn't tilapia sound like a Mayan temple? And how about the orange roughy? It could be a fabric.

Shrimp can be cooked in a variety of ways, but it still seems to retain the look of shrimp.

Then there are the combinations of foods that must come from some remote region of the world that no one ever heard of, like Mongolian russet potatoes mixed with baby eggplant from the Hungarian hinterlands.

You think you may have reached a decision until the waiter appears with the specials.

A trip to the supermarket isn't any better. It took me two hours to figure out what kind of deodorant, eggs and orange juice I wanted to buy.

The deodorant now comes in so many configurations that you have to have a physical before you can decide which one might be OK. I finally chose one that slid on without a fragrance.

The eggs used to be small, medium and large. Not anymore. There are organic, cage-free fed with omega-3, light brown, dark brown and white. I honestly didn't have a clue. What if I chose eggs that are organic, but they put them in cages? Won't that affect the chicken's stress levels? How is that going to be good for me? And don't eggs contain omega-3 fatty acids? What's the point of feeding them what they already have?

The orange juice was the straw that broke the camel's back. There was a time when one orange juice existed: Original Minute Maid. They started by adding the one with pulp. Now we have varieties with some pulp, vitamin C added, no acid, calcium-fortified, and pulp with calcium. And there are mixed flavors: banana and orange, raspberry and orange, mango and orange roughy. Just kidding. But believe me, its coming.

In fact, I think there's no end to what may be down the road. We could be looking at spending an entire day a week making choices. Then we'll have to choose which day we want to do it.

Forget prizes;
Doing right is the best reward

I recently read an advertisement for certificates of recognition for children who achieve certain milestones in their lives.

I will probably be perceived as Fagan from *Oliver Twist*, but the *Rubber Ducky Award for Excellence in a Bath* and the *I Ate a Good Supper Award* make me feel we're going over the edge.

Now, I realize we've come a long way when it comes to understanding the far-reaching implications of all the parenting, but are we now headed towards rewarding people for drooling?

When I was growing up, my mother, who could have doubled for a member of the SWAT team, gave the orders of the day: eat your breakfast, brush your teeth, make your bed, go to school, do your homework, get good grades, don't give me any lip, and go to bed. End of story. There was no cajoling, and if a simple "but" escaped from my lips, my mother would immediately reply, "I'll give you a *BUT,* As long as you are in my house, young lady, you'll do as I say."

Since I didn't have an apartment of my own to run to, or anyone who dared to stand up to what could have been one of the Soprano's alter egos, I knuckled under.

Once in a great while my mother would give me what I'm sure she considered the Academy Award of praise: "That's nice; maybe next time you'll do even better."

I'm sure this message has been at the root of my personality, which is to be a perfectionist. It can truly make you successful, but it can also drive you crazy in the bargain.

Would I be a less neurotic person if my mother had validated me more often? However, much of my humor comes from many of the struggles I went through being the daughter of the hard-driving parent.

Are we creating a society of people who need accolades for the simplest tasks? Does eating a meal deserve a prize, or would you be better off knowing the dangers of starvation?

It appears that no matter what you buy today, you are given points or some plastic replica of something you didn't need. I recently was told that I was eligible for the "bra club". When I reached twenty points, I would receive thirty-three pairs of underpants. Since that meant buying twenty bras in three months, I said, "No, thank you."

The bottom of my pocket book is laden with cards that give me points toward free cleanings, free haircuts, free coffee, and free bananas. How about this? Charge me less when I buy and forget the free stuff because, as we all know, there is no free lunch!

Let's start teaching kids that a lot of what you do in life is because it is the right thing to do, and that is the best reward.

What happened to old-fashioned birthday parties?

So what's up with children's birthday parties? They used to be a simple family function, not much hoopla. The parents, grandparents, godparents, selected aunts and uncles showed up. There was food and a cake. If the kid was really young, you put him in front of the cake, put a party hat on him, and he blew out the candles. A few pictures were taken, the kid went to bed, and the adults continued to eat, drink, and talk. Period, end of story!

When your child went to school, you had a few of their friends over before the adult showed up. Each of them got a horn, a hat, confetti and some silly little trinket. The event included a game of musical chairs and another of pin the tail on the donkey. The relatives showed up, patted the kid on the head, uttered the usual refrain of "Haven't you gotten big," ate, drank, and left.

Enter the new era of the birthday party extraordinaire.

There is a solid month of preparation, consultants from Disneyland, decorators, caterers, and special invitations have to be printed. The child is given a multitude of options. The parents are careful not to replicate anything that vaguely resembles past parties.

After all, the visiting dignitaries must be constantly amused. They could be bored and never come back. Many people choose to have parties at facilities that have sprung up due to this Barnum and Bailey mentality. You can now rent an entire facility where your children crawl through mazes, play a variety of theme-based games, Bippy the Clown sings your kid a song, and then the Marine marching band leads them through town so the mayor can give him the key to the city. All the children in school are invited, plus their parents. The large numbers enable the child to receive hundreds of gift. There is a special chair that has been decorated with gold leaf and dollar bills. A trumpet is sounded at just the right moment and the child begins to open his presents.

This used to be a civilized moment. But something strange has happened. Opening presents now resembles a WWF match: down and dirty!

If you've been to one of these things, you know you could wrap a pair of old socks in newspaper and you'd get the same effect as someone who brought them Macho Warrior or Bimbo Barbie. The poor kid becomes dazed, disabled and disoriented. Finally some adult sounds the alarm — Oh, look, he's overwhelmed and tired. We better take him home to bed.

Yes, the party's over, but there's always next year.

Are we just too busy for good manners?

I've seen articles reflecting on the demise of civility in America. Anyone who hasn't noticed the epidemic of rudeness is either dead or living on top of Mount Everest by themselves. Not a day goes by when rudeness is not only evidenced, but, more importantly, accepted.

I didn't have much choice in the matter. My mother and grandmother were both part of the etiquette police squad, and the nuns picked up the slack. Someone was watching you all the time. This wasn't the simple stuff like saying please and thank you. We're talking about how you ate your soup, how and when you're able to be excused from the table, language that was appropriate, when to speak, and how to listen. The list was endless, but it had to be learned because you were considered undignified and vulgar without your manners. My grandmother use to call manner less people "disgraziate". This means disgraceful in Italian.

Her immediate response to any misdemeanor was to grab her Rosary beads and pray for the transgressor to receive guidance.

Perhaps it's as simple as her wisdom — we have lost our guides. Our parents, grandparents, aunts, uncles, neighbors and teachers were our in-house Emily Post. No one got away with anything!

Did the two-income family start this trend? Is everyone too busy to be a manners drill sergeant? Because that's what it takes: constant drilling. When you're tired from working all day, it's hard to police people.

Did television add to it? It gets harder to instill social graces when a child's role models on television and movies are burping, farting, and scratching their butts while they're eating lunch.

Does the hurry sickness everyone suffers from take its toll? You bet it does. No one has time to be courteous; it takes away from getting to the next errand. It's much more efficient to knock someone over so you can be the first in line or cut someone off so you can get to work three minutes earlier.

Add to the list self-entitlement, which reeks of *me, me, me*, and you set the scene for catastrophes like school and workplace shootings.

I think it's time we all took a look at our own manners and those individuals we have some control over. Let's bring back a kinder, gentler America.

I'd like to see some of the following take a permanent vacation:

- People who chew gum with their mouths open. Personally, I hate gum chewing of any kind.
- Same with eating: don't talk with your mouth full. It doesn't make for pleasant conversation, watching your mouth make mush of your food.
- How about a few minutes of pleasantries instead of "What's up?" I fear for a time when we will simply grunt.
- If you're in the service industry, such as a clerk in a supermarket or department store, don't look irritated because I'm interrupting your conversation with another clerk about the date you went on. Customers are paying your salary.

I'm afraid I could go on for a long time. So I'm going to put the ball in your court.

Casual attire seems to have gone a little too far

Thirty years ago, I took my first plane ride with two of my children to Portland, Maine. We looked like we were going to church, but then, so did everyone else. In fact most people dressed up every day, even when they were just going to the supermarket.

We've come a long way, baby, as they say, since the good old days. Sure, some of that was ludicrous and needed some adjusting. You don't need to pick up a loaf of bread and a gallon of milk looking like you're ready to be photographed for Vogue.

On the other hand, many people have taken the term "casual attire" to the outer limits. My understanding of casual attire is that it covers your body and is less constricting than a suit and tie or dress, pantyhose, and heels. Wrong!

In a recent trip to a local store, I saw many people who perceive "casual" as forgetting to put most of their clothing on. Some could get away with this, but the majority of us need to save that look for having a barbecue in the backyard. Have we gotten so laid back about our attire that we are bordering on the offensive? The more interesting question is, does how we dress affect our behavior and our productivity?

When I was in grammar school, the girls wore dresses and the boys wore slacks and shirts. In high school, we wore uniforms. The nuns held inspections every day: blouses were to be buttoned up to the eyeballs; hems were to be at mid-calf. We had to arrive at school with hats and gloves. Being caught without your hat was a felony.

The FBI could have learned a trick or two from the good Sisters of Saint Joseph.

Over the years, a new paradigm emerged and we became very concerned about people's individuality. We feared that conforming would hinder their creativity and expression of self. People started going to school and work in outfits they deemed appropriate.

Guess what? Not everybody has good taste. Over the years some people's attempts at casual have turned into falling out of bed, grabbing their car keys, and heading out the door.

If you look like you should be in bed, your brain will follow suit. It stays asleep. You become your own nightmare. A long term study on dress and success pointed out the obvious: you take things more seriously when your attire expresses your intent.

Companies are already starting to return to asking employees to dress in a more business-like manner, and schools are cracking down on the so-called *hip* look that often leaves the kids stealing a pair of sneakers that costs more money than a dryer. If they need help getting people to comply, I have a couple of nuns they can call. They'll change those habits.

Have fun despite price tag and bottle caps

For the past several years, I have felt progressively more like the Grinch around Christmas. Perhaps it was the unraveling of my marriage, the pain of a hip that needed replacement, or the feeling that I just didn't want to wander around purchasing more stuff for people who already had too much stuff. This year my holiday spirit was ready and waiting to come out. I am past the grief of divorce, my hip has been replaced, and I decided to celebrate Christmas differently than in past years.

My kids split holidays between me and their in-laws. And because Thanksgiving was our time together, Christmas was left open and available. That's when I decided to invite close friends who might find themselves in the same predicament: with family too far away to visit or otherwise engaged.

After all was said and done, fourteen people showed up. Cooking for that many can be daunting, but I was in a very festive mood and I chose to create an Italian feast reminiscent of my early years, when Grandma Francesca buried herself in the kitchen, chopping away into all hours of the night.

The difference between then and now is that she had no labels to peel off before she was able to use her purchases. I have been trying to figure out what insane individual decided that every tomato, eggplant and other piece of produce needed to be individually labeled with a price tag. Remember the good old scale? You plopped the stuff in and it gave you a price. Not anymore. Now you have to go home and try to remove the sticky little suckers until your nails fall off.

In fact, it goes beyond the produce. I can't think of a thing that I have bought lately that doesn't have a price tag stuck on it. You need lessons in patience to deal with these things so that you don't go berserk and just throw it out.

I love the glassware that has to be soaked, then scraped. After you scrape off the tag, the glue stays on and you have to take a Brillo pad to it to get rid of that. Trying to open new bottles of anything is a nightmare of equal proportions. The basil and oregano jars must have been sealed by the CIA. Do they think there are explosives inside? By the time I pulled off the seal that was sealing the seal underneath, I had a massive headache. But then try to open the aspirin bottle. Everything is childproofed. I know that kids can harm themselves if they get into the wrong thing, but most kids are not going to get excited over eating basil leaves.

More importantly, shouldn't we also be thinking about the older crew whose hands might have a touch of arthritis? Sure, the kids will be fine, but we'll get increasingly gnarled from trying to open things.

All things considered, I came through it all and it added to the laughter and joy we all shared. Don't forget to keep your sense of humor throughout the holidays — it's the best gift you can give yourself and others.

Stop the music! I can't hear myself think!

I stopped to grab a quick bite at a restaurant off one of the local highways, and was immediately assaulted with what I'm sure the management thought was music that would feed my soul as well.

Wrong! It was so loud and so inappropriate to digestion that I was amazed the customers weren't given barf bags to go with their lunches.

Who dreams this stuff up? It can't be anyone who understands what it means to be able to eat calmly while having a pleasant conversation. They must have all been drummers in a heavy metal band for most of their lives.

This seems to be the new hip way to eat: try to outshout the music, and then hope there's a few breaks so that you prepare yourself for the next hearing challenge.

Whatever happened to eating without music, or with some pleasant, soft background music? I imagine that is now only possible in a monastery. Of course, it also could be a calculated plot to get you to eat quickly and leave faster than you normally might so that they can turn the tables over faster.

Or is it because as a culture we have become anesthetized to noise? I realize I may be an anomaly. My friend Nancy says I could probably hear a rabbit running in Iowa. I don't ever remember as a kid hearing music playing in the cheese store, the deli or the corner candy store. Sure, maybe there was some little radio playing some Italian aria or the news, but it wasn't coming out of every corner and you could still hear yourself think.

That's just the point; those in the know figured out that if the music is constant and loud enough you will become mesmerized and buy, buy, buy. If they put the right beat on you can feel yourself flying along in the supermarket, swooping things off the shelves until your cart is heaped full.

Not until you get home do you realize that you bought twenty cans of dog food and you don't even own a dog.

Many of the health clubs I frequent throughout the country haven't figured out the music thing, either. The choices are more conducive to background for a car chase in a movie. Heart rhythms are affected by the beat of the music, so if their goal is to reduce their clientele, they're definitely on the right track.

Music is one of the most magical art forms we possess. It can soothe the savage beast, put a baby to sleep, make a nation feel united, enhance a romantic moment, or make you just want to dance the night away.

The possibilities are endless and the research is there to back it up. So if you're in charge of choosing music for the rest of us, do us a favor. Buy *The Mozart Effect* by Don Campbell, and then go get a hearing test.

Why all the fuss?
It's just a bit of snow

Buying milk and bread seems to be indigenous to preparing for a nor'easter, but why were all the chickens gone?

I stopped at my local market Monday dreaming of the wonderful chicken soup I was going to make to help cure my cold.

The shelves were bare!

The store looked as if it had run a "going out of business" sale. I understand the need for precaution, and I admire advancements in weather forecasting, but I think we have lost our minds. Shoppers were running around like nut bags.

What did we do before Doppler radar and the storm patrols on television that remind us every five minutes that it's snowing? Does all the catastrophizing reduce mortality rates?

I remember as a child waking up to snow. No one knew it was coming; it just showed up. My parents grumbled about the inconvenience of trying to get to their jobs, but they just shoveled the driveway and sidewalk and left. Today, everyone gripes about what a pain it is to have to start up the snow blower.

I walked to school, and it never closed unless the weight of the snow collapsed the building. Nothing stopped the nuns from their appointed task. Their closest rival was the U.S. Postal Service.

If the snow was extreme, say twenty inches or more, everyone stayed home and chilled out. No one became frantic about the piles of "paperwork" they left at the office, or the meeting they were missing.

If the electricity was working, it became a great day to play music, usually opera, and checkers with my grandfather.

I always wished the lights would go out. Then the candles would come out, and I was allowed to light them. My grandmother had a bunch of votive candles and our home ended up looking like the local church.

The end of a storm always saddened me, because until then, it felt as if time were standing still. In those wonderful moments, the only thing that mattered was being together.

Perhaps, that is the "bless" in the "mess". Nature in its wisdom forces us to connect and reflect.

Too much of all things

Remember when chocolate was chocolate — a candy you totally enjoyed? Now it's in shampoo, soap, room sprays and cat litter.

Remember when you drank water because you were thirsty?

Now it's no longer just water. It's flavored and carbonated and jam-packed with vitamins and fortified with nutrients.

Remember when a pizza was just a slice with a pepperoni or sausage topping? Now pizza is a three-course meal in one slice. Stuff is piled so high you need a stepladder to eat it.

What happened to the trendy philosophy "all things in moderation"?

Today, excessive, extreme, supersized and larger-than-life are en vogue. It's ironic that, with all the thousands of self-help books and tapes on the market, even trying to create some simplicity in our lives is more overwhelming than ever before.

Very few of us even bother buying or trying new things out of fear that something bigger and better is on its way — something we simply should not live without.

When the first reality show came out it was fresh and different. Then another one came out. And another. And so on. Reality shows are now the norm, and each is a clone of the previous one — a parody of the original and more superficial than the last. Hopefully, this process will lead into the disappearing process, as what happens with "it" celebrities.

Remember when Roseanne Barr was on the cover of every magazine? She wrote books, had TV shows and appeared on everyone else's shows. She became so visible that she soon became invisible. So much for moderation in her career.

The last thing I read was that Barr was planning a comeback, which will, no doubt, create a new wave of popularity. Ultimately we get sick of her as we did the first time around, just like reality shows. Hopefully, both will end up in the land of been there, done that.

Will life ever return to a time when things were less contrived?

I doubt it.

Not enough people realize that too much of a good thing may just be too much.

Wacky talk
when the right word won't come

I've realized that as we age, or maybe sooner, we begin to create a whole new language for words we can't remember.

My first contact with word substitution was with my mother. Every time we had a conversation, she would discuss a woman who lived on her floor at her assisted-living facility. She began with: "I just talked to what's-her-name."

I always countered with: "Who's what's-her-name?"

"You know," she responded, "what's-her-name."

I used to go through a whole list of questions like an FBI agent looking for an escaped convict: "What does she look like?" "What was she wearing?" "In what area of the building was she last seen?"

Now completely frustrated, my mother made another attempt.

"You know, she always has that thing around her neck."

I would then start to get equally frustrated.

"What thing? What thing?"

Finally my mother gave me a really good clue: "She's got an Italian last name."

Thank God, I finally got it.

"It's Grace Dinapoli, isn't it?" The thing around her neck is a scarf. She always wears one.

"Yes! Yes!" my mother would shout with glee.

The idiotic part of this is that we have had this same conversation about one hundred times and I should have known who she was talking about. But no, I kept thinking maybe there are others who just might fit this description.

I have since come to recognize that most of us go through these moments where words elude us. Most often they're very familiar to us.

On many occasions, I will go around the house looking for "it". I will ask whoever is around if they saw "it".

If they are in the same mental state, they might actually go along with me and ask me where I put "it".

If my mind is in a really bad way, I'll probably say: "It's on the watchamacallit."

This suddenly takes on a life of its own with more insane responses. My son once asked where I last put "it".

And my husband's favorite bit of advice is that I should put "it" someplace where I can find it more easily.

Sounds good, but what difference would that make if I can't remember its name?

His tips always made me feel like I was in a rerun from "The Honeymooners". Only I wanted to be Jackie Gleason and shout: "Just once, I'd like to send you to the moon!"

Maybe it's time for someone to pick up on this whole "other speak". He or she would produce a dictionary for those who simply don't get it so they can understand the rest of us. Then those people could join us and be on the same "whatchamacallit". You know!

Hey, where's the clothing for typical people?

The other day I decided to buy some spring and summer clothing. I thought I'd get a couple of T-shirts and some linen pants.

As I looked through the clothing racks, I began to think that somehow I had stumbled into a store for Lilliputians. All the tops and bottoms were very tiny and very narrow.

The shirts were constructed so that they could expand, but only to the place where they might fit an overgrown troll.

I knew that I could not even attempt to try anything on, since I would need the Jaws of Life to get out of them.

A slim young woman approached me and asked if she could help me. I told her I was looking for a couple of T-shirts in a size 10.

"Oh," she said, trying to hide her dismay, "we only go up to a size 6. Most of our customers wear 1's and 2's, and some are 0's."

"Miss," I replied, "the last time I saw that number was on my children's layettes."

She let out an embarrassed giggle and said, "Well, maybe you can go next door. Their clothing starts at size 10 and goes up to 22. It's the only one around that carries plus sizes."

I thought maybe she was going to add that after I bought my outfit, I might want to get a job at the circus.

Am I the only one who has noticed that clothing is getting smaller and smaller?

If the average woman is five-foot three and weighs 140 pounds, then who or what is buying these ridiculous outfits?

I have seen some poor, misguided souls bulging out of what they perceived was high fashion, but no one I know would be caught dead in them.

I realize that much of the retail clothing market is geared toward the young, but what about the rest of us?

Please, someone help us women who are over fifty. We want to look smart, sassy, classy, and feel comfortable.

That shouldn't be so hard. They just might need to use more material.

There's a lot we don't need to know about each other

Have any of you noticed how much, and how often, we are bombarded with information that we don't really need to know? I'm not talking about the fact that we all want to be aware of news that speaks to global politics, community affairs or health issues. I'm confused as to why the media feels that we need to have explicit information about people's lives.

I don't know how many people reading this column have heard of Greta Garbo. She was a movie star with a need to remain mysterious. Her most memorable statement was "I want to be left alone." Photographers and journalists were obsessed with trying to get her picture into magazines and newspapers. It was practically impossible. This made her even more desirable.

Today it's a whole different story. Most of the celebrities choose to reveal everything about themselves and the lives of all with whom they are involved. It is not unusual to hear a famous star discuss a drug addiction, a stomach stapling or their sex life.

The same thing holds true for many in the political world. We might make some concessions for these folks, because they want to be as visible as possible. However, this need to know has spread into the general population.

As a child, I was often exposed to adult conversation. My grandparents took care of me while my mother worked. Their friends often visited during the day and they sat around for hours, talking, laughing and eating. The discussions often centered on cooking, the national news or some relative who was a little off-center.

But no one offered to reveal the intimate details of his or her life. There was also no discussion of past behavior if it was particularly reprehensible. Everyone knew that certain subjects were taboo and could be considered offensive to those present. More importantly, disgracing yourself or your family was not to be celebrated.

Today it is not unusual to have even a casual acquaintance reveal his or her issues involving incontinence, impotence, possible polyps or how much flatulence they might be experiencing. They also will reveal their incomes and how they are trying to withdraw from eating, drinking or stalking their cat.

It is one thing to reveal something if the intention is to empower those around you. It is unnecessary if it is just to get attention or if it's done for shock value. I think we've all been shocked enough. How about embracing a little mystery? Wouldn't that be more interesting?

Loretta LaRoche

Longing for how life was before things went so high-tech

Over the years I have felt a variety of emotions over the seemingly never-ending march into technology. Nostalgia sweeps over me as I recall having a phone that didn't let people leave a message when you weren't around, but just rang and rang and rang. When no one answered, the caller hung up, resolved to call again or simply forgot about it. You came home to either family, pets or no one. There was no piece of equipment to remind you that you needed to call back or e-mail.

Television, if you had it, was not complicated. Grandma didn't have to take an engineering course to learn how to turn the set on or access more than 500 channels of programming. The shows were pretty simple but a lot of them were fun with stars like Lucy and Desi, Mary Tyler Moore, Milton Berle and my favorite, Sid Caesar. There were good specials by Hallmark Cards — they're still around — and news that was informative and straightforward. No one did their thing wearing little of nothing; sex was alluded to, but there was no frontal nudity or incessant fondling or four-letter words.

Civility also was much more common. Children didn't run screaming through a restaurant as if they owned it, clerks waited on you politely and made you, rather than their co-workers, their priority. I don't ever remember an employee of any establishment talking on the phone while they were waiting on me. There was a lot of saying "please" and "thank you" and "after you", and the gender of the person to whom you were speaking didn't matter. And elders were always respected.

In retrospect, I'm beginning to feel like I'm describing a utopia. We all know that every generation has its problems, and certainly I saw many flaws that have been addressed, adding to our rights as citizens and human beings. But still I find myself vacillating between being deeply saddened and incredibly irritated by how our lives have become so compromised by the gadgets and the so-called hip new value system. I often feel as if we are all going mad.

If Rod Serling were doing a show today, I imagine it might portray a nation of whirling, swirling, feverishly driven individuals walking or driving while on their cell phones, oblivious to anyone around them, while they quickly stuffed a 10-ounce burger and fries down in between shouting, "Can you hear me?" Others will be frantically trying to wind their way through a plethora of androids that sound human until they answer a question you didn't ask. Drivers ranting, horns honking, and phone keyboards clicking away like mad.

Well, guess what? A major credit card company just had an epiphany. They have created a card called Simplicity. It will give you what we all had before for free: access to a real person.

Who knows what will be next. Maybe a store that will train people to recognize that customers keep them in business or a fashion industry that realizes most of us look better with our clothes on?

Try being more civil; you may feel better

I once spent four days in Destin, Florida, doing seminars and visiting my daughter.

What I most love about my work is the opportunities I get that connect me to people from all walks of life, and from various parts of the United States and the world.

What struck me most about the people I met in the Florida Panhandle was the enormous amount of civility they manifested toward each other and whomever they met. I was reminded of one of my favorite movies, "Pride and Prejudice". I love the storyline, but I was always enamored of the graciousness they showed when speaking to one another and their incredible manners.

I often include the value of civility in my talks because I sense its absence more and more.

What I saw and felt in Destin made me feel that I was being nurtured and validated as a human being, and that all I met were totally present when they spoke to me.

I realize that nothing is 100 percent, and I'm sure there are people in the area who don't give a hoot about being civil. But I believe there are fewer than in the Northeast. We seem to be much more preoccupied and invested in the hurry-up mentality.

You can say that living in the South makes life go at a slower pace, but that shouldn't be the excuse or the reason for being rude.

I have often observed road rage on the Southeast Expressway that makes me feel like the animals were let out of the zoo.

I have watched people in the midst of conversations checking their cell phones for e-mail and Facebook updates.

I've seen people's eyes glaze over and watched them literally disappear into the maze of thoughts they are having over what to do next while they are out with friends and family.

I have walked into stores where I felt I was in a self service gas station. I literally had to walk through the entire store to find someone, and when I did they appeared annoyed that they were discovered. When they finally looked up, they gave a perfunctory hello and said, "If you don't see what you want, let me know."

How about these phrases: *Good morning; Good afternoon; So nice to have you stop in; Please let me show you around;* and *What can I do to help you*?

Perhaps we should all take more time to be present to each other, interested, caring and responding to what we're hearing rather than anxiously waiting to get on our way. It might not only reduce stress, but it just might make us feel more human.

Perhaps the real message behind being more civil is that when we treat another as we wish to be treated, we honor not only ourselves, but them as well.

No store can match Grandma's cooking, can it?

Isn't it amazing how many foods are touted as tasting as if they were homemade?

I don't know about you, but I can't honestly say that anything I bought at the supermarket in a can, jar or box tasted even close to anything my grandmother, mother or I made from scratch.

Now, I don't know why we call it "scratch", because I don't think we scratch anything when we cook. What we do is chop, sauté, bake, grill, fry, stir and season to get a taste that no factory can come close to reproducing.

I used to spend a lot of time cooking when my children were very young. Then I became a working mom and meals became a chore. I tried to cook things that were easy like franks, hamburgers, meatloaf and chicken.

But as life became more difficult, I found myself trying things my grandmother would have buried in the backyard for fear of eternal damnation. She hated anything in a can or a box. It always felt nasty to her. One of her greatest fears was that the people who were making the products could have a bad day and take out their vengeance on the contents.

Her marinara sauce was always made from fresh tomatoes and herbs she grew in her garden. She even made her own spaghetti and bread. I realize she didn't work, and that she was fortunate to have a partner who had a similar passion for cooking.

We are obviously much busier today, but I also believe we have gotten incredibly used to food that doesn't taste as good. How can you compare homemade chicken soup to something like Campbell's? They can show an actor serving the soup to a couple whose noses are following the scent all they want, but we all know that it can't come close to grandma's.

It doesn't matter how long a company has been making chili or if they use a recipe that has been in the family for generations. Once it is transferred into a factory that makes thousands of cans a day, it starts to lose something, like flavor. That's why so much store-bought food is loaded with salt and ingredients you need a degree in chemistry to decipher.

So do I think anyone, including me, should be arrested and held without bail by Martha Stewart or Julia Child? No, I just hope we don't become totally invested in not making home-cooked foods. It's so much more than taste. It's the smells that waft through the house, the anticipation of sitting down at the table and taking that first bite, and the joy of approval as everyone licks their lips.

I don't know anything store-bought that can replicate that experience.

Silence is a quality too long forgotten in our world

Whoever said silence is golden is long gone and so are his words of wisdom. Essentially, the idea of silence falls on deaf ears.

Over the last twenty or so years, noise has become more and more a part of our culture. I thought about this as I sipped my coffee at around 7 a.m. surrounded by a tsunami of sound. There were leaf blowers whirring, hammers pounding and various landscaping trucks going up and down the street in front of my house.

I try to enter my day slowly and in somewhat of a meditative fashion. Maybe it's a throwback to my days as a student in a Catholic boarding school or perhaps I have, as a friend stated, "ears that can hear a rabbit run in Idaho". Who knows? What matters to me is that the world is becoming a noise factory, removing us from ever being able to hear ourselves think or to enjoy such subtleties of sound as birds chirping, a gusty wind or clocks ticking.

We seem driven to distraction by televisions blaring or iPods nestled in our ears, playing songs at decibel levels meant for the hearing-impaired. Audiologists are reporting that the younger generations will experience deafness much sooner than their parents or grandparents. This has got to be apparent to anyone who goes to the movies. I have left theaters that had the sound cranked to such a degree that I thought I was witness to a space shuttle taking off.

I realize that technology has created things like surround sound for us to have the effect of "being there". But couldn't I "be there" without feeling as if I have to put my hands over my ears? Obviously, I am falling prey to sounding like my mother, because a lot of my grandkids look at me as though I just stepped off Noah's Ark when I start my noise lectures.

I often wonder what would happen if a law were passed that required everyone to engage in one day of complete silence each year. Could any one of us manage to do it? Somehow I doubt it. Most of us have a need to blah, blah, blah all day long. It might be interesting to try it, though.

Recently a film called "Into Great Silence" was released. It's about the lives of the white-robed Carthusians who live in the most rigorous and ascetic monastic order in the Western world. Filmmaker Philip Groning waited fifteen years before he was allowed within the walls of the monastery. He lived the life of a monk as well as filming the two-hour, 42-minute film. It is a film virtually without sound. I intend to see it from the perspective of challenging myself to just be with the silence. Believe me, I have to work hard at this just like so many of you. I can be a real mouthpiece if I don't "watch my mouth", as my mother has so often pointed out.

You may want to go to the movie with a group of friends and see how it feels, or you just might want to think about how much noise you've allowed into your life, and how it adds to your stress levels. If none of the above appeals to you, then so be it. But make sure you have your hearing checked periodically because you may be losing one of life's most precious commodities and not even realize it until someone is talking to you and you hear nothing but silence.

When you cheat, you deceive yourself

Over the years, a vast amount of media attention has been on people who scam and cheat their way through life. It's done within companies, on school tests and, yes, even among family members.

Has cheating become more prevalent? I happen to think so.

Maybe because I remember a time when if you did cheat, you were considered a total disgrace by your family and friends. I went to Catholic school, and the nuns would stand in front of the classroom with eyes that had laser beams for pupils. When it was test time, they would go over how the test had to be taken and what would happen if anyone was found with a cheat sheet. They would periodically go up and down the aisles, their black robes swishing and their rosary beads clanking. The combination of fear of them and fear of eternal damnation was enough to make you afraid to move in your seat.

Once in a while someone would turn his head to look at a classmate, only to have a firm hand placed on his shoulder. The sister's voice, soft but stern, would say: "Is there something you need?" That was enough to bring the hairs on your arms into an upright position. It took just one reprimand; from then on, your eyes stayed focused on your paper.

Of course, the fear they instilled was only one piece of the pie. My mother was the other piece. If she had been told that I had cheated, she would have had a field day inducing guilt.

"Is this the way I brought you up? Every day I work like a dog so that you can grow up and be a successful human being!"

I suppose many people would consider this kind of training to be somewhat like boot camp. Yes, it was rather daunting. A lot of information has come to light about not threatening children with fear tactics because that can lead to neurotic, anxious adults. I believe there is definitely truth to this mindset.

However, along the way, the need to succeed, make lots of money and be able to buy the latest, greatest stuff has become more important than having a conscience.

There is also the issue of pride. I was told that if I cheated, I gained nothing but the knowledge that I couldn't rise to the challenge.

Today, you can go online and get the answers to tests. There are websites devoted to cheating. I'm sure there are other, more sophisticated ways that have emerged of which I am not aware. You might even be able to wire yourself like an FBI informant and get the answers from a truck hidden in an adjoining neighborhood.

Anything is possible. But what I do know is that your self-worth is more about the rewards you receive from the efforts you put into whatever you do. In the end, we may be able to fool those around us, but the one person we can't fool is ourselves.

Women's underwear: The tool of torturers and sadists

I'm really beginning to hate underwear! As I've gotten older, my body seems to be saying, "Please, let's just wear a muumuu with nothing underneath." I have searched far and wide for underpants that don't ride up or grab me and hold on like a vise.

I remember my grandmother wearing pink bloomers that seemed so large, they could have doubled as a tent. She must have known something because I never heard her complain that they bothered her.

Bras are even worse. The underwire was definitely created by a sadist intent on leaving his mark on every woman who wears them. I can't be the only woman who feels like this because the ultimate relief that most women seek is taking off their bra.

What if every woman in the world took off their bra at the same moment? You would hear a groundswell of happy sighs.

I don't know if men have the same issues about their underwear. It might make for an interesting panel discussion.

What really amuses me is the latest plethora of underpinnings to hit the stores that are supposed to help you look thinner.

There's the control-top half-slip aimed at slimming your waist, tummy and thighs. That's a big order!

I know for a fact that if you have extra weight, all these garments do is push it to another area, making you look like a sausage that's been tied in the middle.

There's something called a thigh tamer. When did thighs need to be tamed? Do they come with a trainer and a whip?

If you are too thin, they have padded panties to give you a "bootylicious look". I know I'll never need those.

There are so many choices, but most are based on looks, not comfort. Maybe my grandmother had the right idea. Her underwear didn't control anything. It was just there, and she controlled it.

At your service? Not so much anymore

Last week, I traveled throughout New England doing seminars and shows with one of my best friends.

We drove and stayed in four places. It was a hectic schedule, but we always have a great deal of fun because both of us are able to laugh quite easily. There was, however, something different about this trip. We noticed a significant lack of customer service at the inns and restaurants. I have witnessed a downward spiral over the last several years in the service industry.

Many stores I walk into seem to be inhabited by clerks who are more transfixed on talking to their co-workers than trying to discover why I walked through the doors. I have circled many shops waiting to see if anyone will ask me if I need help.

When I approach them and ask for a particular item, they often respond by saying, "If you don't see it, then we don't have it." There isn't a "Let me see if we can find it for you" or "I'm sorry you're disappointed." They just merely go on with their conversation as if I disappeared into thin air.

I've been amazed by grocery clerks during checkout having constant dialogue with the person bagging the groceries. The only time they stop and talk to me is when they can't figure out what one of the fruits or vegetables is called because they've never seen it or eaten it. You would think that once they heard what it was, it might make them inquisitive as to what you do with it. But no, they just pick up the conversation where they left off, and I'm left standing there waiting for the next trivia question about something else they've never seen.

In a few of the inns we visited, the owners appeared lobotomized. One stood at the door as we struggled up the stairs with our suitcases. He said he had to make sure the door stayed closed because there were wasps in the vicinity. Meanwhile, it might have been better to be helped and stung than have a heart attack dragging the luggage.

I've had many wonderful experiences over the years and met some attentive people who are in the business of serving the public, so I know they still exist. But I fear they are becoming a dying breed.

Our interactions with real people are diminishing and being replaced by voice mail, androids and e-mails. People's lives have become so overwhelming that treating others with dignity and respect is losing value.

I don't know how it's going to end up, but I do talk to myself more now than ever before. At least I know one person is listening.

Remember writing? Today's communication is bad for our brains

Does anybody remember writing letters? I used to write them all the time as a child, especially thank you notes. My mother was a dog with a bone when it came to thanking people. Her litany was always the same:

"If they bothered to buy you something, you can bother to thank them."

Writing as I knew it started to change with e-mails. Correspondence became more pointed. Then text messaging emerged, and with its birth a new language was born — one that is almost absent of language.

"R U OK?" "Wassup?"

I think back to my Catholic school education and the good Sisters of Saint Joseph, and wonder how they have dealt with the demise of their beloved vocabulary. Not a day went by without a daily dose of new words and exercises in writing that focused on incorporating their use.

My mother was equally vigilant about words. She felt that a day without learning a new word was a wasted day.

She absolutely hated what she called filler. "Umm" made her twitch. I would have to put five cents in a jar every time I used it.

"Umm" is still around, but another filler has been added which seems to permeate a lot of conversations. It's the word "like". I used to think it was mainly relegated to young kids and teens, but I've heard a lot of adults use it as well.

"It's like that", "Like, whatever you want to do." I can understand that each generation creates rituals, clothing and euphemisms that relate to itself, but "like" doesn't seem to want to go away.

It's hard not to notice it when it's every fourth or fifth word.

I know Sister Mary Immaculate would have probably made the individual write, "I will not use the word 'like'" three or four hundred times on the blackboard. I don't know if teachers can do that anymore. It did seem to make a lasting impression.

What's really fascinating about all this is that our need to expedite communication and how we're doing it is going to have an effect on our brains and, therefore, our relationships. If you don't use it, you lose it.

Language creates emotion. Using less vocabulary and writing in shorthand might seem efficient, but in the long run it is the wonder of words that adds richness to our lives and our relationships.

Endless quest

I used to love my pajamas. Then menopause hit and I found myself feeling like I had somehow been left stranded on the Sahara Desert every night.

Most often I would sleep in the buff, but then I would suddenly feel like an Arctic wind had enveloped me and I would frantically whip the pajamas back on.

As a result of my body's relentless changes in temperature, I decided to embrace nightgowns. You can whip them on and off in one fell swoop. I had never really been crazy about them, except for when I needed them for those "special occasions".

Some nightgowns are supposed to be alluring and provocative — something you don prior to what could be a night to remember. They're a part of the art of seduction, along with candles, music and whatever else floats your boat.

As I got older, I found that my body was shifting and I started to think that maybe I should replace the so-called "teddy" with a shroud. The thing is, shrouds are for unveilings, and I really wasn't in the mood to unveil anything.

My quest for the right nightgown has continued. The goal has always been to stay cool and comfortable. Even though menopause is a thing of the past, it has left reminders: hot flashes that seem to come periodically in the night.

Over the years, I've tried sleepwear that's short, long, medium and mini, and made of cotton, silk, bamboo, flannel, spandex or a combination. I've investigated possible choices in countries I've traveled to — Australia, for instance. There, I was thinking that perhaps some Aboriginal woman had found an ancient material capable of transitioning from warm to cool in an instant.

No such luck.

After initial enthusiasm, the outcome is always the same. As long as I don't move, all is well, but unless you're a corpse, tossing and turning is part of sleeping.

Most often, my nightgowns turn into pythons wrapping themselves around me like tourniquets. They're usually somewhere around my neck, trying to choke the living hell out of me.

So, naked may be the only option. If I hear my cat howling in the morning when I get up, I may have to think of something else. Let's see what happens.

Don't stop giving encouragement:
We all could use an occasional pat on back

Yesterday I went to a local restaurant and as I left, I went into the restroom to wash my hands.

The room was filled with at least seven women in a circle, surrounding a little girl who couldn't have been more than two years old. Each of the women exclaimed how wonderful it was that the child had sat on the potty and performed her duties.

Over and over the accolades continued, followed by applause. I couldn't help but laugh as I thought of how often children are applauded for the simplest of things, like going to the bathroom, taking their first step or saying their first words.

As we get older, the applause lessens.

Let's face it: when was the last time you got a standing ovation just for sitting on the toilet, walking across the room or just saying "Hello"?

As children, validation and encouragement are par for the course, unless of course, you have been surrounded by individuals who didn't have the ability to do so.

I was blessed with a family that thought much of what I did was fun, and they would display my precocious ways to anyone who would watch. However, there came a point where my mother in particular would chastise me for the very things she thought were cute and adorable.

Her favorite mantra was: "You're just too much. You can't be acting silly all over the place. What will people say?"

My teachers, the good Sisters of St. Joseph, would constantly tell my mother I was bright but liked to laugh too much, and, in addition, would try to make other people laugh as well.

The good news is that I never stopped either of those traits, and ended up making a living from them.

Over the years I have found that many individuals forget their childhood exuberance in lieu of becoming adults. They often become terminally serious.

We all need applause, and often for the more mundane practices in life.

Get your co-workers together and give each other standing ovations for coming in to work.

Applaud your husband or wife for making breakfast or just getting out of bed. Clap for the clerk that bags your groceries, or for the hygienist that cleans your teeth.

Sounds crazy, maybe, but I think if we all applauded each other more often, there would be a lot less anger and hostility in the world.

Progress marches on, sometimes in reverse

We've all heard the expression "Leave well enough alone." Unfortunately, the 21st century lifestyle does not seem to want to embrace this concept.

I certainly am of the opinion that we should try to improve things so that they are more productive and efficient.

However, over the years, some things that were just fine were replaced, but what was thought to be better wasn't necessarily so and would certainly make some people very rich.

Take water, for instance. We used to drink it out of the tap, then "they" (whoever they are) decided tap water was probably contaminated and started bottling it. Eventually millions of people bought trillions of bottles of water that they kept with them 24/7 in case of a possible drought.

Now the latest, greatest revelation is that the bottled water is worse than the tap, and the plastic bottles have BTA in them, which is a carcinogen. There is also the problem of getting rid of these bottles, which pose a threat to our environment.

Years ago, everyone went to the store with cloth or net bags and put their groceries in them. But "they" decided paper or plastic was much better. Now eco-friendly enthusiasts are recommending we go back to cloth bags, and some supermarkets are banning plastic.

Paper towels replaced dish rags to wipe up spills. Well, rags are coming back, especially since sponges have been accused of harboring enough disease to kill an entire nation and paper towels are ridding us of our tree population.

What do you think will come back next? Not common sense — that you can bet on. My guess is washboards.

Get rid of your washing machines. We'll use less water, and using a washboard could even tone your upper arms.

We ought to focus on humanity's bright side

When I was in Vancouver last week, I came upon the work of a wonderful Japanese artist, Yasuo Araki. I was very taken with his work and purchased two small paintings that reflected his greatest passion: helping to bring peace to the planet. His works often have heart shapes with angel wings or motifs such as the stars, the sun and the moon.

Mr. Araki was 6 years old when he and his family fled from the B-29 bombers that rained explosives down on his country. It led him to believe that his mission in life was to try to communicate peace in all that he did.

I have often considered myself privileged in what I do because I am given the opportunity to meet incredible individuals who have somehow survived their lives and gone on to do amazing things with what they have learned from their own pain. I feel there are many people who have somehow risen from the ashes to lead their lives with grace and dignity.

Some make a difference by their mere presence and how they conduct their daily activities without the histrionics our culture is used to. Others choose to be more visible, like Dana Reeve, who took over her husband's legacy and continued on, even though she was suffering from her own illness.

Unfortunately, our culture chooses to showcase the dysfunctional, the bizarre and the violent. Many talk shows feature guests whose lives resemble some underground cretin culture. Why would you even want anyone to know that you had thirty children by twenty different men or that your boyfriend was really your mother dressed in drag?

When I was growing up, those kinds of things were considered the skeletons in the closet. Now, the skeletons are not only let out, but they're made into the movie of the month. My grandmother was a maniac about protecting the family name. She should have been in the CIA. Nothing about the family went beyond her kitchen. If you behaved in a despicable manner you were told up front. You didn't need to go on Maury Povich so that an audience could reprimand you.

I don't know about you, but I think it's time somebody did a show that reflected the many decent, honorable and heroic people that inhabit the planet. I'm willing to bet there are more of them than those who are ready to audition for the next version of "Mad Max".

If we continue to focus on the dark side of humanity, we will find it more and more impossible to see that there is a light at the end of the tunnel. I wish to take this opportunity to thank all those who e-mailed or wrote me their thoughts on what made them happy. Keep them coming. They were uplifting, poignant and profound, and most importantly, filled with light.

Chapter 4

Living a Juicy Life

"Always be a first-rate version of yourself, instead of a second-rate version of somebody else."

~Judy Garland

Pursuing genuine happiness is worth the effort

I have embarked on a very interesting journey.

I am taking a 24-week course called "Authentic Happiness". At the end of the program, I will be certified as an authentic happiness coach.

Some may consider this a frivolous concept, but trust me when I tell you this: there is a huge body of research in neuroscience and psychology that shows positive emotions can alter brain physiology to lift depression, enhance immune response and help one to be a happier, more successful individual in all areas of life.

Who among us has not been asked this question at some point in our lives: Are you happy?

But what does it mean to be truly happy? Our culture strives to make us feel that we cannot feel good unless we have the latest and greatest product being touted on the airwaves. Money is supposed to make you happy. So are finding the right person to live with, being healthy and having great children, among many other things.

But it appears that there are three things you need to do to be genuinely happy:
- Be aware of bringing pleasure into your life every day, particularly through gratitude.
- Be fully engaged in life by being connected to something that brings you so much joy that time has no end and no beginning.

- Discover meaning and purpose so the world will be a better place as a result of you being in it.

Most of us would think that embracing this sort of philosophy would take too much time. After all, we have to keep moving and doing and getting things done.

Much of that may be true, but then the question is this: do we simply want to live life as if we are on autopilot, constantly reacting to daily demands, rather than realizing that we can create better experiences for ourselves, our families and the world if we just take the time to be more fully engaged?

I don't know about you, but I think feeling truly alive takes work and, more importantly, courage. It means that we not only notice people, places and things that make us happy but that we also comment on how wonderful they make us feel. Most of us are great at complaining and criticizing. Why not make a concerted effort every day this week to tell someone how much they mean to you or how thankful you are for any effort they have made on your behalf?

It costs you nothing but a few extra minutes, and the benefits could transform your life.

Children's view of life is magical

Whenever I am with my grandchildren, I am reminded of how magical life can be. The younger ones seem to infuse their lives with creativity and imagination. They instantly become animals, princes, princesses, robots and dragons. It is truly compelling to watch them transform into a character with whom they have become enchanted. They grab whatever they find and turn it into a sword, crown or cape, not worrying if it isn't the right material or shape.

Their inner critics have not been solidly formed, so they are not inhibited by voices that remind them that their imaginary journeys are a fool's paradise and that they should be doing something much more productive.

Unfortunately, most adults have lost their connection to the world of imagination and mystery. They become serious and overly practical, feeling that make-believe is a waste of time.

Yet we yearn to reattach ourselves to those magical years. Just look at the success of books and movies such as the *Harry Potter* series. It is not just our children who are obsessed with this phenomenon; we are all a bunch of silly Muggles. While our grownup world dictates that we need to work, work, work until it is all done, our spirits yearn to connect to whimsy, delight and fun.

Much of the stress we feel comes from not incorporating these childlike concepts into our lives. If we allowed ourselves to be more childlike, we would eat less, play more and, ultimately, be in better shape. Instead, our days are full of stress and we stuff ourselves with food to ease the pain. Why not try to reclaim some of the magic we've left behind? Rediscover it in books, movies or simply by rethinking some of the imaginary journeys taken as a child and sharing them. Don't let it go. It is what infuses life with energy and what makes it divine.

Resolve to share your time

One of the best resolutions that you can make, any time of the year, is to give the gift of yourself. Volunteering, sharing or caring for a friend or family member not only lifts the spirit of the other person as well as your own, but it may even help you to be healthier.

As I grew up in Brooklyn, my home looked like Grand Central Station. People came and went, and some never left.

No one was homeless back then; they all stayed with us. The characters that came and went are part of the tapestry of my life. They live on in some of the conversations that my mother and I have had over the years.

No matter what time of day or night, there was food waiting and someone to share it with. I have so many fond memories of my grandmother's chicken soup and her tiny meatballs in hearty sauce, which, she was convinced, could cure just about anything. There are thousands of individuals who have been the recipients of Francesca's healing foods.

If anyone in the neighborhood was ill, the word went out and the entourage would immediately show up with baskets of food, words of cheer, and assurances that prayers would be said for a speedy recovery.

Today, you are lucky if you get one night in the hospital. You call a cab, go home and get into bed, and pray someone will find you if you've dropped dead before the coroner show up.

Why not spend a few hours here and there to give of yourself? Involve your children. It is one of the best ways to help them not to become entitled.

Stop in and welcome a new neighbor.

Pick up some flowers and leave them on a co-worker's desk.

Next time you're depressed, think about the last thing you did that was kind and compassionate. Then enjoy the calmness those thoughts inspire!

Enrich, don't just entertain

In my grandparents' generation, free time was spent in ways that were enriching.

I remember my grandfather would sit around in the evenings and listen to Italian opera on the radio. He would read Pirandello. Every day he'd go out and buy the Italian language newspaper and he'd read every word. And he was not unusual in any way. He was not particularly well-educated or intellectual for his time. He was an ordinary working man of his generation.

In those years, in the absence of television, people spent their leisure time pursuing forms of entertainment that were enlightening and that stretched their intellect. It's hard for people to do that today.

In a society like ours that is so overworked and overstressed, when we finally stop working and want a few minutes to unwind, we do the thing that is easiest: we turn on the tube.

That's not necessarily bad. Listen; there are things that qualify as good television. There's even a particularly funny woman on PBS from time to time, so far be it from me to trash the medium.

I think that there are very important and powerful dramas being produced today. There are excellent documentaries and cultural programming. There's some brilliant comedy that is cleverly entertaining and fun to watch, and there are even a few talk shows that stimulate and actually enhance people's lives.

The point is that we need to make intelligent choices about the way we are entertained. If we allow ourselves to get drawn into the seductive, lowest common denominator programming that is very aggressively sold to us as entertainment, soon, our intellect will be pulled down to the lowest common denominator.

By entertaining ourselves with things that are stimulating but not intellectually reaching, such as one thousand dollar quiz shows or bite-fast talk shows, we increase our feelings of spiritual emptiness. We fall into a tempting trap; it's pleasurable to spend time in a mindless way. When your mind is engaged all day, every day, it is relaxing to let it be simply immersed but not really entertained or challenged.

But it's deadly. In our hearts, we all know that what we are doing with the time is, really, just wasting it away. How often have you even heard people use the phrase they "killed a few hours" watching television?

I don't know about you, but I don't have enough hours on this planet to want to kill any of them!

You can't take it with you

When I think of the pressures advertisers put on consumers, I think of my elderly aunt who is ill and housebound, and watches those home shopping channels day in and day out.

I swear, she is quickly going through bank accounts buying stuff she is never going to use.

She buys little trinkets to beautify the house — new small appliances that I doubt she'll ever use (she doesn't cook gourmet meals, so why does she need a set of twenty-two Japanese knives?).

She buys lovely pieces of jewelry, but she never dresses to go out. She is clearly living out a fantasy, one in which the sad things in her life are forgotten about in the pleasure of opening boxes full of pretty new merchandise.

That pleasure center in her brain keeps wanting more and more, and cubic zirconia necklaces clearly fill the bill.

Luckily, she has enough money so she won't end up on the street because of this habit, and in the last days of her life, who wants to take this pleasure away from her?

So she continues to sit there with her remote control and the telephone at the ready, looking for something to buy. But for me she is symbolic of everything that is wrong with the way we buy today. She is a victim of our consumer culture, sitting on her deathbed, hoping for redemption and pleasure through the things that she buys. I don't know about you, but I'm damned sure that I don't want to spend my last days like that.

Take some time and ask yourself the following questions:

- Look through your closets: do you actually wear the clothes you have?
- Are you seduced into buying something because it's a bargain, even if you don't need it?
- How often do you make sure that you actually have the money to pay for an item before you charge it to a credit card?
- Do you search the bargain tables incessantly? Just what do you think you're going to find there, and is it really worth the time?
- Can you ever remember feeling that you were just going to die if you didn't get some new product? Now stop and think about it. What, really, was so important?

Keep in mind that shopping is often a way of filling emotional needs that are not being met. When you have the urge to shop 'til you drop, take a deep breath, relax and try to concentrate on what it is you feel you're missing.

More often than not, it's nurturing, validation and love. These are items that cannot be found in any store. They are basically there any time through you, or through friends and family. And the good news is they are free.

Stand up and resist the epidemic of apathy

In the past couple of weeks, I have had many an in-depth discussion about how frightening the world feels at this time. Not a day goes by without a report that points out some form of deception. We learn that major corporations falsely report their incomes, that drug companies proclaim miraculous results from products that have not been tested thoroughly, and that religious beliefs are being tested and trust in those who represent God has been seriously compromised.

Our feelings of safety have diminished since the Sept. 11th terrorist attacks left us with the recognition that we are as vulnerable as any other nation on the planet.

Television and radio are filled with programs that seem to show people in their most debased state. And the music industry tries to persuade us that a young rap star called Eminem, who degrades women and rants about killing his mother, is akin to the prophet Moses of the 21st century.

I imagine many of you have had similar sentiments. And why not?

Sometimes it feels a little like the downfall of Rome. As an advocate of optimism and humor, I try desperately to seek ways to counter this sensation of being part of a culture I think has lost its footing.

Perhaps we all need to look at ourselves and try to figure out how we developed into a society that is so incredibly invested in entitlement, rudeness, greed and a propensity for turning anything bad into entertainment.

The most primitive cultures seem to know that individuals who are immoral and indecent are considered outcasts from the tribe. We give them book contracts, put them on television and make them household names.

Why do we watch shows that we know are not only stupid but also nasty?

Why don't we all write letters to our government leaders showing our disgust at how many individuals' lives are being ruined by major corporations who insist on giving their CEOs enough money to build their own towns?

Ranting to each other does nothing. I am fortunate to have a platform to show my disgust and to encourage each and every one of you to begin taking a stand.

Don't become part of the epidemic of apathy. Don't watch junk TV. Garbage belongs at the dump, not in your head. Join an organization that seeks to make positive changes. Whether it be the government, the environment, abuse, drunk driving, or the homeless.

Do something! You have the power... use it!

The power of words

We are losing ground in the vocabulary department. While e-mail is quick and efficient, it has downsized our language skills.

This is particularly disturbing because our brains are deeply affected by our language. Choosing different sorts of words changes the patterns in our brains. That's the amazing power of language. It makes sense intuitively, doesn't it?

If someone asks how you're feeling today, and your answer is always a mindless, "Oh, fine," how do you think that contributes to the way you feel? It keeps everything on an even, if boring, keel. It rules out enthusiasm, energy and vitality. It keeps the heat at room temperature. It helps the brain make sure that, indeed, you feel kind of mindlessly "fine".

But if, instead, you could be specific and descriptive about the way you feel, it would honor the emotions inside you and help your brain define and respect them. It would give shape to the wide range of your feelings and the more you understand your feelings and repeat their language, the more you'll give yourself room to feel them. It would fill you with energy and enthusiasm to live life to the fullest — to really feel your feelings.

Think about the words you use. Do you act like you're in a vast field of wildflowers with the sun shining overhead, or are you stuck in a ditch with no way out?

Here are some wildflower words: joyful, delightful, encouraging, challenging, hopeful, creative, insightful, playful, whimsical, relaxing, amazing, brilliant, amusing, courageous, brave, bold, respectful

One of the ways I encourage people to shift into a more positive state when they're having a tough day is to use words that are incongruent in relationship to the problem. Instead of saying "I'm having a terrible day," add one of the words from above. For example, greet a colleague with the following statement: "I think this is going to be a brilliantly horrible day."

Or if you're feeling gloomy tell people you're feeling "delightfully depressed". It puts a whole new spin on things. It gives one a sense of playfulness about problems instead of making everything into a crisis.

Get out your dictionary and learn some words that can add power and attitude to your life. Share them with your family. Our lives can be incredibly enriched or diminished by our explanatory style. Some of my fondest memories are of evening meals where my mother would insist that I share a new word that I learned that day.

Language is one of our greatest gifts; make sure you are aware of it every day.

How can we be bored? There's so much to do

I have never been able to understand how people live their lives repeating each day as if it were stamped in permanence.

They eat the same thing for breakfast, go over the same dialogue with family and friends, moan and groan about their job, the traffic and the awful things that are happening in the world, eat dinner without much fanfare, then go to bed, ready to continue the next day where they left off.

I realize that they might very well be happy. Who knows — they even might be in a state of bliss. Perhaps seeking, exploring and being filled with curiosity about what is possible in this limited time we have on Earth is a curse. But frankly, I'll take being cursed.

Ever since I was a kid, I have been completely blown away by what we humans have been given as gifts on this planet.

My biggest problem has always been what I perceive to be not enough time to do all the things I want to do. Whenever I hear someone say, "I didn't know what to do so I went shopping," I think, "What are you, nuts?"

When's the last time you took a walk around a gorgeous pond or a hike through the woods? Have you been to a museum lately, or a concert? Have you cranked music that you like and wildly danced around the house?

Imagine how many wonderful dishes there are to cook. How about joining a book club, learning an instrument or taking dancing lessons?

You may have passions you stored away when you were a child in order to become a serious, responsible adult.

So many people have been drilled with messages that take away those things that fill you with joy and fun. I honestly think some people get stressed out because they are incredibly bored with themselves.

We're constantly given messages that when we find the right partner, we will be fulfilled. This is a disastrous way to live life. No one can give us what we need to give ourselves an interesting, juicy life.

In fact, the more exciting we are, the more the chances are of meeting exciting individuals.

Getting divorced was difficult but it has also provided me with the ability to go back in time and revisit interests that I had thought I would never have time for again. Two weeks ago, I started taking ballroom dancing lessons at the Fred Astaire Dance Studio in Hanover.

When the music came on and we began to do the steps, I thought, "I'm in heaven."

I hope to keep going and — who knows — maybe even get into a competition. I might take piano lessons, study yoga or learn to speak Chinese. So many exciting possibilities. Auntie Mame said it the best: "Life's a buffet and some poor suckers are starving to death." So get going, before your time is up!

Resolve to not resolve

With every New Year's Eve comes the expectation that we should make some resolutions for the coming year. For most people the top priority seems to be losing weight. I would like to offer a different type of outlook for the New Year, one that is predicated on discovering what *is*, rather than feeling the negativity of what you haven't accomplished.

I suggest you begin a joy journal. Joy is not about guilt, anger, bitterness or resentment. It comes from inner peace, the ability to give and receive, and the ability to appreciate. It is a feeling of gratitude for the gift of life.

Keeping a joy journal will help you maintain a feeling of elation, the sense that you're soaring with the eagles instead of scratching in the dirt with the turkeys. Starting your day out by writing in a journal seems to reduce stress considerably. It makes perfect sense, doesn't it?

Most of us start our mornings by reviewing everything we have to do, and all the things that might go wrong throughout the day. This type of behavior becomes a habit. And habits are hard to break, especially ones that don't serve our best interests.

For some reason beyond my understanding, we humans seem to enjoy making ourselves feel worse than we have to. If you're hard-pressed to know how to begin with a daily dose of joy, then let me try to help you with the following suggestions:

1. Think of a person or persons who have really made a difference in your life.
2. List three or four things that you do well.
3. Write down at least ten things that you like about yourself.
4. Think of a time when you had so much love in your heart, you could have burst.
5. Think of your favorite physical activities as a child (hiking, swimming, skipping rope...). List them, and make plans to do them again.
6. Think of five qualities that you adore in your partner or spouse. Write them down, and tell your significant other about them.
7. Think of a time when you felt supported in a time of need. Describe it and how you felt.
8. Remember three times when you felt inner peace and serenity. As you recapture the feeling, write it down.
9. Think of someone you might forgive and how that might change your life.
10. Who do you laugh with the most? Remember a time you laughed so hard, you thought you might collapse.

There are literally hundreds of things that give us joy. Make this a year filled with joy, joy, joy!

For more self-esteem stop talking, start doing

How many of you out there suffer from "put-off-itis?" You've got it if you keep telling yourself you're going to do something and then keep waiting for the right time and place to do it.

As a kid, I would often try to get out of doing things I was supposed to do. My mother had an insatiable need to keep the house clean. Every Saturday, no matter what, we had to vacuum, change the beds and clean the bathrooms.

This was the case even if it looked like it didn't need to be done. It was the rule. And my mother pretty much stuck to her rules. She didn't care if the pope was coming to town; you had to clean the house.

When I would protest, which I did quite often, she would tell me to just "put it in third gear" and get going.

"Once you get it done, you'll feel better," she said.

When you're a teenager, that kind of rhetoric doesn't make any sense. Why would I feel better? My mind told me that just going out with my friends was going to make me feel better.

Over the years, I began to recognize what my mother had discovered throughout her own life and was trying to share with me. Getting to the end of a task — whether it's cleaning the house, going to the gym or doing your homework — gives us an unbelievable sense of self. Thinking about doing something or talking about it endlessly does nothing but make you feel like you're treading water. It also gets old and tiring and starts to make your friends and family think you're always just "blowing in the wind".

Many of us are adept at thinking about what we're going to do rather than doing it. Oh, yes, I think dreaming about stuff and hoping it's going to happen is fun. But that's never going to infuse you with the same energy and joy that accomplishing what you're thinking about does.

I have found that the only way I can keep challenging myself to do things that I might just talk about is to jump into the fire and see if I can avoid being burned. My love of cooking has returned, and to stoke the flames, I invite friends over for a meal. When I'm in the middle of it, I think, "What am I, nuts?" But then I hear my mother's voice and I know she's right — do it and you'll feel so good when it's done.

Going to the gym, losing weight, cleaning the closets, visiting cantankerous relatives, whatever it is that feels difficult, will jump-start your self-worth in ways you can't even imagine.

So get going, even when the going gets tough. Anyone can do the easy stuff. That's why it's easy.

It takes true grit to get through life, and that takes practice.

Try hard not to be someone who strives joylessly

Over the years, many people have told me how lucky I am to be able to work at a job I love. And believe me, I wholeheartedly agree.

I get to interact with thousands of people from all over the world, see places I would never have imagined visiting and hopefully get to make a difference to those to whom I speak.

These past two weeks I experienced one of the highlights of my career. I got to do three events in Canada with former President Bill Clinton.

He spoke about how often we are told how lucky we are to do what we are doing. Yet what many do not understand is that luck has very little to do with creating a life that is authentic to who you are and what you stand for. So often when I am teaching a workshop, participants share with me their frustrations over being unhappy about what they are doing with their lives.

It is so interesting that we often accept a half-empty cup in areas of our lives that speak to work or relationships. Years of our lives are spent earning a living, and so many feel trapped, waiting for the day when their time is up, like a prisoner marking the days behind bars. Others suffer through marriages that serve neither spouse because of guilt or lack of financial security or not wanting to be alone.

It is astounding that we spend so much time teaching skills like math, geography and science and so little time on teaching life skills. What if we all learned how to develop amazing communication skills or how to create those things we are passionate about, starting in the first grade? What if we learned how to set goals, be tenacious, accountable and responsible to ourselves, because we are worth it?

Instead, much of what we choose is often about what others want. Parents sometimes try to influence their children according to what they missed out on in their youth. The kids become the alter ego. We have seen this occur more and more in sports, where parents go ballistic when their child doesn't make the cut.

I realize that obligations and a host of other issues often get in the way. But at any stage in life we still have the capability to make life changes. If we never get the life we truly aspire to, life has a way of getting us. The stress that comes with feeling unhappy with your existence can be life-threatening. It is also exhausting. I call it joyless striving.

Take some time to think about how to live an amazing life. It will be the best thing you ever did for yourself.

You never know, so act on your fondest dreams today

My career has taken me to many wonderful places and today I am lucky to be going to, of all places, Monte Carlo. This is a very special trip because I am going with my daughter, who is in remission from non-Hodgkin's lymphoma. When she was diagnosed, we made a pact to make sure that we would always stay in touch!

Over the years I have heard many people discuss their hopes and dreams. They have ranged from healing relationships with loved ones to climbing Mount Everest. At first, I would simply accept their excuses as to why they couldn't do what they wanted to do. We all do it, don't we? It's so much easier to find reasons not to fully engage in life's possibilities than to jump in and test the waters.

I realize that there are considerations and certain times of life that require extreme responsibility. But, that being said, I believe that there are two reasons we don't execute some of our dreams;
1) We're afraid, or 2) We delude ourselves into thinking we have more time than we do. It seems that nothing cancels out that thought as quickly as being told that you have an illness that could reduce your years on the planet. Suddenly, all the excuses go on the back burner and living life to the fullest becomes most important.

I think getting older has somewhat the same effect if you have the strength to think about it. I feel somewhat possessed to do all I can to be with those I love and to have as much fun as possible. I hope that, as you read this, you might reflect on what it is you yearn to do or say and not waste any more time just thinking about it. Thinking can help to begin the process of "doing".

But we need action to make things happen. Call someone today that you may have problems with or need to forgive. Visit a travel agent and begin planning that trip you've always wanted to take. Take care of your health. Increase your ability to be happy. Say "yes" to life every day.

My mother's favorite saying was "You never know." I could never figure out why she said that so often. But now I know. I hope you do, too.

Instead of being fed up, try seeing the good

How many times a day do you think you discuss or think about negative issues in your life or someone else's life?

I have often suggested to my clients that they tape their conversations for one day to observe how much energy they expend making themselves and others crazed and humorless.

How does your day start? Do you begin by announcing how you wish you could stay in bed longer, how tired you are or asking why the weather isn't better?

Do you follow this rhetoric up with more of the same throughout the day?

When talking to a friend, significant other or co-worker, is your conversation sprinkled with negative opinions about other people's looks, behaviors or actions?

Have you ever compared your energy level when you're not whining and complaining to when you are? If you have, you may have noticed that you feel and even look better when you're not talking about what's wrong with everything and everyone around you.

I'm not a simpleton who thinks we can go through life without discussing events or people who bug us. Some of it is healthy. If we thought everything we did and everyone we were involved with was fabulous, we could find ourselves in many compromising situations.

I've noticed over the years that whining has become a national pastime.

If you watch television for a couple of hours or skim through magazines, you will feel yourself being flooded by information about a host of things that could be wrong with you.

The list is endless: too hairy, loss of hair, diarrhea, constipation, social anxiety, depression, nail fungus, hammertoes, relationship issues, lack of self-worth, clutter, wardrobe disasters, weather, kids from hell, toxic parents and more.

You could have any one of these problems or all of them. And if you do, you can bet there is a medication or program to help you — but not without the side effects, all of which are listed. Confusion sets in and you wonder if being screwed up is better than the cure.

The news channels like CNN spend hours reporting every problem that is occurring on the globe at any given moment. You can feel good but in minutes fall into despair about a monsoon in China. I appreciate the possibilities of being globally informed and I know that I can shut off the television, but I would just like them to spend an equal amount of time telling us about what's good about the world.

How about infusing us with hope and a sense that humanity is not doomed to dry up and blow away as a result of not drinking enough water?

The bottom line is that it all starts with us. Try to spend more time appreciating your life rather than getting aggravated by it. Share good news with your friends and family, even if the only thing you can think of is that you're breathing.

And if something really bothers you, do something about it. If you can't, learn to accept it. Try to keep the cup full and overflowing. It will help you have a long, juicy life.

Getting unstuck

One of my favorite films was *Lovers and Other Strangers* because it so reminded me of my Italian family. But what I loved the most was the insistence the father had in trying to find out why his eldest son wanted to get divorced. No matter how many times Johnny tried to explain why he wanted out of his relationship, his father would interrupt by saying, "So what's the story?"

Essentially, the father did not want to hear what his son was sharing. His need was to have him stay in his unfulfilled marriage, because no one in the Vecchio family ever gets divorced.

That was his story and he was sticking to it.

Over the years, I've heard countless people talk about why they are unfulfilled, have jobs they hate, children who don't listen, spouses who are indifferent or health issues they haven't got time to take care of.

Over time, people compile a body of evidence and experiences that make up their storyline. They reinforce the storyline by telling it over and over to all who will listen. They eventually convince themselves that the only possible ending is the one they repeatedly focus on.

It always amazes me how we can convince ourselves that not feeling OK mentally or physically is preferable to getting unstuck. I can understand it to some degree, because I have fallen victim to my own novellas. There is an element of safety attached to a familiar situation, even when it doesn't serve our best interests. How easy is it to just keep gaining weight, even though we know we may be compromising our lives?

Standing up for ourselves is much harder than making sure we don't make waves, and staying in situations that don't feed our souls in any way because they're safe may feel easier than taking a risk. However, the mind and body eventually reach a level of intolerance, and you may find yourself feeling anxious, depressed or coming down with more physical ailments. Essentially, the human spirit thrives on being authentic.

As I've gotten older, my biggest regret is that I spent too much time and energy on stories that should have ended after the first page. My hope for myself and all of you is that we can use our wisdom to go forward and create new stories that end up being best-sellers.

Check unhealthy baggage: Dragging the past along fails

So many of us get caught up not just in trying to find out who made us stressed and miserable, but also in storing the information and cataloging it for future use.

I call this "baggage handling" because after a while, we have so much past misery that we need suitcases to put it in. We may even need to hire someone to carry them if we have a whole set.

My grandmother, Francesca, was so good at recalling history (mostly negative) that she could have been a curator for the Smithsonian. As a child, I would always ask her why she looked so unhappy. Her answer was always the same: "Because I suffer."

She'd go no further, but her face would become even sadder and her hands would go up in the air as she recited one of her many invocations to God to help in her hour of need.

There was always an aura of mystery around my grandmother's suffering, as if it were so unspeakable that it could only be alluded to in veiled words. Every once in a while she would add a teaser: "My mother abandoned me!" This was all said in Italian, which added incredible drama. If she had said "My bra is killing me" in Italian, it would have sounded like a death knell.

So many of us spend our energy keeping lists on file of things people have done to us. It's as if we have to keep a hold onto everything that once made us feel bad.

Women are particularly adept at this. Our partners and children don't have a chance if they repeatedly do something that gets on our nerves. We can come up with dates, times, and probably the exact minute they did it before.

It is important to know when to let go. There is nothing more liberating than releasing old stuff.

I realize today that some people who have been part of my life were energy vampires, and ruminating over how they treated me did not change their essential character. The only logical thing is taking that experience as a lesson.

Life can hold a lot of joy and possibilities, but only when we stop dragging the carcass of the past along with us.

Where does the time go?

Every day we are assaulted with demands for our time. Significant others remind us to take out the trash, bring the clothes to the cleaners, make an appointment for the dentist, and get the dog to the vet. Children need to be transported to games, helped with their homework, and reminded daily about their responsibilities. Family members need phone calls and visits, and the media blasts messages about not forgetting Mother's or Father's Day. When all is said and done, our lives hold little availability for our own dreams or for our ability to create ways to take care of ourselves.

When was the last time you sat down and wrote a list of what you value most?

Whenever I ask a group of stressed-out people what they hold dear, "family" is universally first. We've all been told that this is the noblest response. Who among us has been told to put others before yourself? Or to remember that family is everything?

Not thinking this way borders on blasphemy.

But I'd like to stimulate you to think a little differently. You should be at the top of your list. If you are not taking care of yourself, you cannot expect to take care of anyone else.

I grew up with a parent who constantly told me how hard she worked and how exhausted she was as a result. Her metaphor for her existence was "I work like a dog."

That statement both amused and saddened me. My irreverent mind imagined a dog going to work in a suit and high heels while my guilt button was ringing off the wall. How many of us hold the people we love hostage to our constant messages of "Poor me, I don't have any time for myself because of all the sacrifices I'm making for you"? It doesn't even have to be said. It shows up on our faces and in our body language.

I always felt that I was the cause of my mother's lack of time for herself. The flip side of this constant litany is that I made a vow to myself that I would never choose a career that made me feel like a prisoner.

We all need to realize that becoming mentally, physically and spiritually well should be our top priority. When we are in this place, we stop looking to others to fill the well. Imagine a culture of individuals who really pay attention to self-care: productivity would go up, paychecks would increase due to less monies going into disability and medical care, anger and violence would diminish, and altruism would become a way of life.

And then we could all have more fun. What a concept!

Reach out and seize some joy, one day at a time

Who among us is not familiar with the phrase "carpe diem" (seize the day)? I don't know about you, but personally, I don't want to seize anything.

However, I do want to squeeze the juice out of every moment of every day. I would love my days and yours to be filled to the brim with delight, joy, love and good humor. Life often takes on its own direction with constant demands and expectations that make us forget what we are really here to do with the time we've been given.

One of my books, which came out in May, is titled "Squeeze the Day". It contains 365 ways to bring juice and joy into your life. I would like to share twelve of my favorites:

1. We live in a world of excess, in which how much we own defines who we are. I'd rather *be* too much than *buy* too much. It's much easier. I'll never have to have a yard sale to get rid of myself.
2. If life hands you lemons, you could become bitter or you could make lemonade. Frankly, I'd rather just throw the lemons out and get something I really want instead.
3. In order to be fully alive, you first have to be awake and aware, otherwise you're simply sleepwalking.

4. If you're always trying to be right about everything you do and say, you'll soon find that you have no one around you that's interested in how right you are.
5. Try to make a difference in the life of someone less fortunate than you, because one day you may take their place and they may take yours.
6. Know that if you allow others to be themselves, then you can stop focusing on trying to clone yourself.
7. If you can laugh every day, especially at yourself, you've found the best joke in the world.
8. If we all moved more and ate less, the diet industry and the food police would go out of business and we'd all have more money to just have fun.
9. If you have children, allow them to see you as their parents. They already have friends. What they need are mature adults who set limits, teach values and are responsible citizens of the world.
10. Keep in mind that nothing is written in stone but on your tombstone. If you're flexible, you can change your mind, your plans and the direction of your life. If you're not, you might as well live underground.
11. Stay conscious of the fact that people around you can hear your cell phone conversations. Find a private place to talk, if possible, or speak more softly. Most of us don't care that you closed the deal, finished your workout, got the

kids to soccer practice or finally made it to the grocery store. Enough already!

When you're flying down the road and you've missed your exit, just be grateful it's not the final one!

Chapter 5

Lighten Up!

"The shortest distance between two people is a smile."

~Victor Borge

We really shouldn't waste the humor all around us

I did a show this past weekend with three of Boston's best comedians. As I waited to do my bit, I was able to do something I never get to do, which is to listen to other really funny people. After each person finished, I questioned him on where he got his material.

They all had the same formula: observe the human condition.

I, too, have found that nothing is funnier than reflecting on the absurdities that we all involve ourselves in without realizing that we have become the joke.

The material the comedians delivered was filled with experiences of the sort that all of us have had, like the Big Dig, relationships, weight loss, children, mothers and more.

But most people would rather make themselves nuts than see the funny in the person or problem. Granted, not everything is funny, but a lot of life is very much like a Farrelly Brothers movie.

I often wonder why so many individuals choose to create a drama around their day rather than a sitcom?

Wouldn't it be great if we could all be trained to be stand-up comedians? I think the skills are there from the beginning.

If you watch children, you're bound to see a Jerry Lewis, Carol Burnett, or Ellen DeGeneres in the making.

Unfortunately, we think comedy and laughter are appropriate only after all the serious stuff has been taken care of. That's wrong, but by the time you realize it, you're close to taking your last breath.

Nothing makes life more like being on cruise control than a bunch of healthy guffaws. Imagine if you were trained to be able to turn an argument with your mate into a scene from a funny movie.

What if, in the middle of your tiff, you said: "Wait a minute. I'll be right back. Hold that thought."? And when you returned, you were naked except for a large red bow around your waist and a rose between your teeth.

What would happen if you wore a funny hat on your head or a red nose when you took your kids somewhere? Oh, they might feel odd about having you as a parent, but they'd get over it. And what stories they would have to share as they got older and had their own children.

How about going food shopping in a boa or a funny wig? Imagine the fun you'd have in the deli line.

I'm sure most of you would rather have bamboo shoots under your fingernails than take my suggestions.

However, the point is that many of us are doing just that: torturing ourselves with angry or irritating thoughts, rather than titillating ourselves with humor and a sense of playfulness. Give yourself a break, lighten up and you'll lighten your load.

Forget conformity:
Try painting outside the lines

I don't know about you, but I think our compulsion to fix everything "wrong" with us is making the world an awfully boring place.

You know what? If Edgar Allan Poe were alive today, he'd probably be enrolled in an anger management program, and then we'd never have "The Cask of Amontillado" or "The Raven".

Van Gogh would likely be a guest on Dr. Phil, where the host would try to reunite him with the woman for whom he had cut off his ear.

What a lesser world it would be if Rembrandt, Picasso, Dali, Michelangelo and Emily Dickinson had spent their lives memorizing self-empowerment rituals instead of practicing their art and expressing their pain.

What a wonderful place we'd be at if our culture could stop obsessing over what we do wrong and ways in which we don't fit the mold and, instead, focus on laughter, connection, play, meaningful work and creative individuality.

Instead of trying to persuade us to fit in, wouldn't it be nice if we lived in a society that encouraged uniqueness? Remember being a teenager, when the idea was to try to appear unique? We all tried so hard to stand out from the pack, to get ourselves noticed. It's something that seems to be indigenous to adolescence; that comes out of a genuine need to display creativity and individuality.

Even when teenagers take part in what seems to be a trend, they put their own spin on it. Isn't it sad that the impulse to be different somehow gets lost? We all try to conform instead. Wouldn't it be wonderful to honor both human impulses?

In the best of all psychological worlds, we would find a way to allow ourselves to be and feel unique while not doing things that are so bizarre that they intimidate others.

For me personally, I try to spend as much of my life as I can with characters. You know, the people who really stand out from the crowd, who see things differently, who dare to look and act different, who behave eccentrically.

I'm drawn to people who not only break the mold, but pulverize it. David Weeks of The University of Edinburgh in Scotland conducted a major study of eccentrics and discovered that they live longer, happier lives. His study revealed that because eccentrics ignore societal norms, they have more optimistic outlooks and less stress.

So seize the day, and paint outside the lines.

Talk to me
(if you've got anything
interesting to say)

In every way, it feels more and more as if we're all floating past each other in our own plastic bubbles. We say things that repel people rather than draw them in. Instead of conversing, we perform soliloquies. Even in a lot of big mainstream movies, there is no dialogue anymore; it is reduced to short, snappy lines that sound as if they've been written, rewritten, and then edited twelve times by professional comedians.

We are getting the signal that conversation is boring when, of course, the truth is that conversation is the glue of life. It can be the most fascinating, intense, enriching and exciting way to spend a few hours.

But it takes time.

Conversation is about listening to another person and then responding to and engaging with that person. It's about opening up lines of communication, not shutting them down. And we do that by talking about subjects that will interest the other person and make them want to talk to us.

Narcissistic subjects end conversations. Reconsider if you find yourself relying on these subjects in conversation: things you eat, things you don't eat, what you drink, what you don't drink, how tired you are, what time you go to sleep, how much exercise you get, how much fiber is in your diet, how hard you work, how much weight you gained or lost, your cholesterol level, how long you can last on your Stairmaster, and/or what vitamin supplements you take.

It amazes me how often these subjects are the source of conversations. They're so mundane, so boring. Yet time and time again, I sit with people and these are the things we end up talking about. It makes me nuts.

Engaging subjects are about things that go beyond just the basic food-and-shelter subjects just mentioned.

Listen, it's not so surprising that you ate today. If you ate standing on your head, now that might be worth sharing. Most people go to bed, but sleeping in a closet might be worth talking about. Shopping for food in your local market is pretty ordinary, but if you bought Mandarin oranges in China, then talk to me.

Move your priorities from the back burner to the front

In the last several weeks I have questioned many areas of my life. It is not unusual for me to do this because I am extremely introspective and curious.

The events of the past several weeks have escalated my need to re-evaluate how and what I'm doing. I imagine many of you have embarked on a similar journey.

It always fascinates me how life takes on new meaning when we are threatened personally or globally.

Loretta LaRoche

Why does it take the possible loss of life to begin to really treasure it?

Many of us seem to go through life as if we are hypnotized. Our daily activities become so predictable that we become our own Groundhog Day. We cannot deny that there is safety and security in knowing what comes next, but if this is the case, why have so many people recently announced that they are no longer going to wait to express love, to connect more, or to live life to the fullest?

The answer is quite apparent: we no longer feel as if life will go on as usual. The irony is that life has never been predictable. No one is born with a lifetime guarantee against pain, suffering or death.

All the exercise, healthy eating and meditating will not stop the inevitable. We can protect ourselves to the max, build a concrete bunker in the backyard, and still someday, our life will end.

This is in no way meant to create a sense of morbidity, but rather to encourage you to make sure the resolutions you made either to yourself or your family and friends in the wake of the Sept. 11th tragedy do not fall by the wayside.

A quote from the Talmud states, "If not now, when?" This ancient wisdom should connect with us daily.

Review your life to see if it meets the criteria for a joyful existence. My sense is that most of us are not celebrating enough. We keep waiting for a special occasion.

Stop waiting! Buy some party hats, horns and some confetti and keep it in the car or on your person. We don't think twice about blowing the horn if someone wants an extra two seconds when the light turns green. Try being festive whenever you can.

When you get impatient, whistle, hum, or sing softly to yourself. Greet people enthusiastically as if you haven't seen them for years and you miss them desperately. Have dialogues with friends and family about what can be done to create more peace in the world instead of reviewing the horrors day in and day out.

And stop talking about what's missing in your life. You probably could do it in your sleep. Instead, begin to create what you need. A happier, more contented you might help change the world for the better.

Martyrdom habit can be a tough one to break

Do you feel that you're constantly taken advantage of? That you deserve nothing and need nothing? When someone asks you what's wrong, do you answer, "If you loved me, you'd know."? If so, then you are suffering from martyrdom.

Martyrs run around trying to take care of everyone and everything, and then they tell everyone around them about how much they've done and how, if it wasn't for them, nothing would get done. The end result is that they seethe with resentment. And the people around them cringe when they see them coming.

I doubt if martyrdom is genetic, but it does run in families. It seems to pass from mother to daughter in particular. My grandmother was the queen of martyrdom. She wore black in case somebody died.

I positioned myself as a martyr for years because I believed that my friends and family would simply adore me if I did everything possible to make them happy. I even thought of starting a new religious order, the Sisters of Perpetual Responsibility. After all, when you're so good and decent, you should eventually be canonized.

Guilt often drives a great deal of this behavior. We somehow have been left to feel that we have never quite made the grade, and so we strive endlessly to find someone who will finally say, "You're terrific. You can rest now."

Unfortunately, most of the people around us are used to having us do everything, so they do nothing. It eventually becomes a vicious cycle. You do it all, they watch you do it, you get angry, then they get mad because you constantly tell them they don't do anything. Now everyone is tense and it becomes impossible to have fun and relax.

If you're part of the martyr model, try to break the pattern by doing the following:
- Tell people what you want; don't accuse them of what they're not doing. For example: "I'd like you to clean your room by 5 o'clock today," not "You never clean your room." They already

know they don't clean their room; you've told them a million times.
- Make sure you take time to "just enjoy". We hear this statement a lot. Saying it is one thing, acting upon it is more important. In fact, studies done on 96 volunteers by Arthur Stone, PhD, a psychologist from the State University of New York, found that pleasant events gave a boost to the immune system that lasted for two to three days. They also discovered that the absence of ordinary pleasures may take an even greater toll on our health than stress does.

So try to give up your mantle of guilt and martyrdom. You are not going to get extra points for suffering unnecessarily. Remember, you don't have to be a doormat — just go to the store and buy one.

How was your day? Full of clichés?

I walked into one of my favorite eating establishments the other day to have lunch with my son. When it was my turn to order I began by asking the woman behind the counter how she was. She responded by saying she was OK, but it was just one of those days.

Over the years a slew of clichés have arisen that we use to define how stressed we are. I know you've all heard them or used them yourselves. But you probably have never looked at them from a comedic point of view.

I imagine that the writers who developed *Seinfeld* could have made an incredible show out of "It's just one of those days."

What kind of day is "one of those days"?

My interpretation is that it has been filled with one problem after another, and it's been awful. I asked the clerk if she ever has said, "It's not one of those days. I feel great." She said she had never thought to do that.

Think of some of the other clichés like, "It's going to be a long day." What exactly does that mean?

Every day consists of 24 hours as far as I know. People who are overwhelmed have determined that they have longer days than the rest of us.

If they were enjoying themselves they would say, "Doesn't time fly when you're having fun?"

So, a long day means stress and struggle and a short day is about fun. Shouldn't we reverse the situation and express our days differently?

How about this: "It's been such a long day filled with fun and laughs." Most people either wouldn't get it or would think you're on drugs.

One of my favorites is, "You just can't imagine!" Then the body language kicks in. Their eyes roll backward and their shoulders tense up until they look like a vampire's victim. They usually don't give an explanation, so you're left trying to figure out what dark and sinister things have happened to them.

Did they fall into a ditch on the way to work and have to dig their way out with their bare hands?

Did they try to shave their legs only to find more hair than when they started?

Maybe when they opened the lid of their triple latte, a giant bat flew out screaming, "It's going to be one of those days!"

Who knows? But more importantly, wouldn't we be better off sharing some of our brighter moments with each other? We have all been influenced by people's moods. And moods are created through our conversations.

You don't have to make any great efforts to change. Just be yourself. But try to keep in mind that life has many elements of a sitcom, and we're all part of the cast.

Faulting others is faulty

For years, my family was caught up in discussing who did what and when.

Many of the good deeds people performed were lost in the quagmire of finger-pointing and self-righteousness.

We sure do love to rattle off what others haven't done, while we religiously recount how we would never do that! Then we go into how much we have done for others and what day and year we did it.

Perhaps the oldest historian in the family was my mother, who had massive lists on everyone. She could remember when I took my diaper off and what I did with its contents, how I kept her up at night, how many hours she worked to send me through college, and how I broke her favorite wooden spaghetti spoon.

Mind you, she broke it when she smashed it on the table after getting mad at me for "behaving foolishly".

My mother probably could have used a couple of trunks for her baggage at this point and a few Sherpas to carry them.

I used to get upset about her capacity for negative recall. I would counter by defending myself, desperately trying to deflect what I thought had brought her displeasure with what I thought might bring her pleasure.

This was usually a no-win situation. I always felt that, no matter what I did, it was never enough.

Eventually I came to realize that my mother's greatest wish was for me to be a happy, successful human being. I now know that she was doing the best she could with the information she had on parenting.

Unfortunately, many of us suffer from the illusion that if we continually point out the perceived flaws of those we love, somehow, they will miraculously change.

Wrong!

No matter how many times or in what context you criticize, it does nothing but make the other person become more resistant to whatever you suggest.

Some of us are born with incredible needs to control everything and everyone. I have struggled with this for years. I now know that I should have criticized less and praised more. The acorn does not fall far from the tree.

However, this takes a higher level of self-worth. I was less sure of myself when I was younger, so when I saw someone as less competent, it made me feel more satisfied about myself.

This is not the path to a higher self. My hope is that we can all discover that it is far more nurturing and a lot more fun to catch someone doing something right than it is to catch them doing something wrong.

Try it. It could become the most powerful thing you've ever tried.

A sense of humor helps us cope with life's absurdities

I find it hard to believe that so many people tell me they don't laugh as much as they used to.

I know that life brings us its inevitable ups and downs. However, if you're not in the midst of a monumental crisis, laughing should be easy.

You may be thinking, "Easy for you to say. You're naturally funny." Well, there's a lot of truth to that. I have a natural propensity to be able get others to giggle and guffaw. Practically everyone in my family was comedic. So, genetics does have something to do with it.

However, I believe we can hone our sense of humor by using it regularly. It gets rusty when we toss it aside because our lives are focused on the serious task of getting through the day, as if we were waiting for the parole board to give us time off for good behavior.

The best way to get laughter to be part of your daily existence is to become more observant — not in a way that creates another job, but more as a witness to the absurdity that is available in many areas of life.

One that always cracks me up is the many drug commercials in print and on television. We have become such a nation of pill-poppers that there is a medication for practically every condition known to man. Too much gas and bloating, indigestion, diarrhea, impotence, hair loss, menopause, toe fungus, scaly, itchy skin, flaky scalp, allergies, yellow teeth, hammertoes and wrinkles are just a sampling of what comes across our screens almost every day.

I'm beginning to think there is some plot by drug companies to create a nation of hypochondriacs. You almost feel as if there's something wrong with you if "nothing" is wrong with you. The other day, my friend, Susan, sent me an ad she thought I'd really get a chuckle out of. She was right.

One of the biggest complaints people have is problems with sleeping. There are medical conditions that create the inability to sleep restfully, but a lot of it comes from the stress people impose upon themselves. A mind filled with "awfulizing" about what has to be done cannot shut down.

And so, the latest, greatest antidote is something called Sleep Well. I love the name. Sounds very "Winnie the Pooh". Curl up with your blankie and Winnie and embrace the wonders of a restful sleep. The ad says that it "not only helps most people fall asleep fast, but it helps you sleep all through the night, peacefully, uninterrupted. It works quickly, so you should take it right before bed."

When else would I take this medication if not before I went to bed? I don't think I would take it right before I went to the supermarket. Unless I want to be found snoring in the vegetable aisle. And the best part of this drug is the safety concerns: Sleep Well may cause drowsiness. DUH!

If you need more stimulation to laugh, I suggest going into the laxative section. But don't take it until you get home.

P-s-s-t:
Try something "unsafe" once in a while

I was very fortunate to have a mother who pushed me to be curious and passionate about life. Whenever I showed an interest in something, she would encourage me to try it.

I can honestly say that I was blessed with an entire family of curious people who were not interested in living life inside the proverbial box. It was almost mandatory to try things.

I was told more often than not that I needed to be interested in learning about many things and not try to be "just like everyone else".

The problem with that philosophy is that it makes waves when the people around you are hell-bent on living life each day in the same way.

I realize that some people feel safe in this context and that we all have a certain degree of responsibility to live up to.

That being said, we can all integrate variety into our lives so that we can be interesting and vital people.

The brain needs the stimulation of change; otherwise it starts to wither like an old piece of fruit.

The first step to developing a mind that embraces possibilities is to not get overly invested in believing everything you think.

Try to step back and ask yourself what it would be like to try a different approach.

What would happen if you didn't have the same cereal for breakfast every day? Or if you took a different route to work, or actually asked someone who differed with you to explain his opinion without getting defensive?

I don't know about you, but I do not want to exit this world knowing that I lived my life as if I were a robot.

I so often wish that I had another fifty years on this planet. I can only hope that I, as well as all of you reading this, keep the flames of curiosity alive in yourself and your family members.

I leave you with a quote from the poet Mary Oliver: "When it's over, I want to say: all my life I was a bride married to amazement, and I was the bridegroom, taking the world into my arms."

Laughter can be a way of life if you're aware

Every time I do a seminar, people ask me how I got to be so funny and how they could see more humor in their own lives.

The answer is a little complicated.

For many years, I have studied how humor and optimism can reduce stress, and I'm convinced of the following:

- Some of it is brain chemistry. There are individuals whose propensity for music makes them incredibly talented. If our families encourage our abilities, we are in luck!
- It's your perception of humor. Do you find it hard to laugh because it makes people think you're not serious enough or professional?
- Are you aware of what is going on around you and how comical it can be, or are you so self-absorbed — "busy" — that you can't focus on anything else but your "to-do" list?
- Are you depressed or anxious, a state that diminishes your ability to laugh and enjoy life? We may not all have the genetics, and some of us may be struggling with our biology (i.e.: mood disorders).

- If most of us were fully present to life, we would laugh a heck of a lot more. Just a simple exercise like reading the newspaper can turn into a comic feast if you allow yourself to read some of the stories that are not about the horrors in the world.

For example, an article I read recently had a headline that immediately pulled me in: "Airline Passengers Spot Flying Monkey".

Now here's a man who boarded a flight to Fort Lauderdale from Lima, Peru, with a fist-sized marmoset under his hat and perched on his ponytail. Security did not see the monkey, and the flight attendants did not see it either. A passenger spotted the monkey and asked the man if he knew that he had a monkey.

Once discovered, the monkey spent the remainder of the flight in the man's seat and behaved itself. No monkey business for this little guy.

I was cracking up while I was reading this. There are sitcoms all around us, but most of the time, we're just more interested in "catastrophizing" and "awfulizing" some minor irritation.

I'm going to see if I can get a monkey to take on the road with me. Maybe he can carry my luggage. I could even buy him an accordion and get him to play and sing "That's Amore" on board.

Now that might help some passengers get the monkey off their backs when they are upset about delayed flights, middle seats, or long bathroom lines.

Find ways to enjoy your life

Several years ago, while attending a conference on wellness, I was struck by the participants' attitudes.

Most of the attendees approached the sessions, which were focused on how to extend life, with grim earnestness and very little energy. Their faces looked as if they were getting ready to go to a funeral. In their relentless pursuit of a long and healthy life, they had forgotten the joy of being in the present.

One afternoon, a child of about three years waltzed down the hotel corridor, twirled, lifted her arms and yelled, "Ta-dah!"

Several adults stopped dead in their tracks. At that instance, I knew they had grasped the absurdity of the situation. The child knew what they had paid hundreds of dollars to find out: how to enjoy life in the moment.

A child-like "ta-dah" blesses the moment you're in. It permits you to enjoy wherever you are and to realize, more often than not, that you choose to be there. If you fail to understand this reality, then you are forever waiting to "be done" before you have fun.

There is even a scientific study that concludes that throwing your arms into the air can lift your spirits. A study by Dr. John Cacioppo, an Ohio State University psychologist, says that it may have something to do with the fact that this upward motion is similar to bringing food to the mouth, an action we instinctively enjoy.

The giddy, goofy desire to throw your arms wide open and embrace life not only makes life worth living, but may make it last longer. Perhaps euphoria is good for the body; perhaps joy is protective against the corrosive impact of stress, and joyful people may outlive their whining counterparts.

There is even a yoga pose called Tadasana, which means "stand firm, with power and dignity, steadily and comfortably."

There are endless possibilities to enjoy our existences. Life's little pleasures too often disappear from our busy days.

The absence of ordinary pleasures may take an even greater toll on our health than stress. So trade frowns for smiles, turn on your imagination, talk to yourself in fun ways, try to be different, tap into the universe of humor, use your good towels and eat dessert first.

And forget trying to make lemonade out of lemons. Throw those lemons out and get what you really want.

Caregivers

Tomes have been written about how to say "no", which seems to plague women more than men. We're beset with the "pleasing sickness".

Too often, our friends and family members perceive us as the eternal caregivers. Once we've taken on the mantle of Florence Nightingale, we become best known for our "nursing" skills and are constantly called upon to help others. Most of us who exhibit this behavior also try to get people to recognize how well and kind we are by refusing to accept help ourselves.

This stoic behavior reeks of martyrdom and will often begin to rankle everyone else because no one can really give and give without showing resentment.

Eventually, others will turn a deaf ear to our whining about how oppressed we feel. It's a no-win situation.

I can remember a time when I "had" to take care of others because I thought that was the only way I'd be appreciated or loved, but that's never the way it works.

Doormats are simply something for people to wipe their feet on. If you're a consistent people-pleaser who often feels taken advantage of, try the following exercise:

Put a forlorn expression on your face and slump forward so your body looks hunched over. Then say the following in a pitiful voice: "Whatever you say is alright with me. I don't need anything for myself. I'm just here to do whatever I can for you. I hope you'll be happy with me. After all, if I can't make you happy, my life is meaningless. Maybe someday, someone will care about me."

Repeat this dialogue over and over for about three minutes and then see how you feel. Of course, you may feel absurd, but it may also get you to think about how this sounds to the people around you.

I suggest the next time you feel you can't say "no", respond with, "Let me get back to you on that," or "I'm going to take some time to think about it." Or try my favorite: "I'm feeling confused right now. I'll get back to you later."

Mohandas Gandhi said it best: "A 'no' uttered from the deepest conviction is better than a 'yes' merely uttered to please, or worse, to avoid trouble."

The good things in life never end

There are days I find myself overhearing conversations where someone is talking about how horrible his or her day has been. More often than not, the conversation concludes with, "It never ends."

I wonder if there's anybody on the planet who has not used that phrase. It's highly unlikely because it appears to be the universal statement for getting and expecting the worst life has to offer.

And, usually, it isn't even about something really tragic. It could be a series of events, like getting a cold, being stuck in traffic, finding out your kid failed gym, and having your husband tell you he's having seven guys over to watch football.

Sure, each of these situations could be irritating in and of themselves. Having them all come together in one day is certainly a test of one's patience. But it doesn't require us to create a huge drama resembling the suicide scene from *Madame Butterfly*.

It seems that most of the conversations we have throughout the day are devoted to making ourselves appear as if we are the victims of a global plot aimed at making our lives difficult. Why we are not attuned to reporting our joys or the incidents of humor that we might have observed throughout the day?

Does that only become possible when something really awful happens, so that we finally have a comparison to our mundane complaints?

I would hate to think that it takes real tragedy to discover that life is pretty good most of the times. Didn't we all witness the surge of gratitude for family, friends, co-workers and life itself in the weeks that followed September 11th?

Can it be sustained, or are we slowly falling prey again to finding what's wrong every day instead of what's right? I think it takes a conscious effort to look on the bright side, and it's somewhat the same as deprogramming someone who was a cult member.

Our minds *can* be trained to think differently.

Start tonight when you go to bed by telling yourself that you'll be in a good mood when you wake up tomorrow, and then think of ten things that made you feel good during the day.

When you wake up, throw your arms up into the air and shout "I'M BACK" Greet your family with a smile. And give compliments whenever possible.

And the next time you think of saying, "It never ends," add it to the end of a sentence filled with joyful happenings: "I'm breathing, I'm walking, I'm employed, I slept in a bed, and I have on clean underwear — it never ends."

Chapter 6

We Are Family

*"1. Be impeccable with your word.
2. Don't take anything personally.
3. Don't make assumptions.
4. Always do your best."*

~*The Four Agreements* by Don Miguel Ruiz

Mangia, mangia! Food was the center of family life

I watched a program on PBS recently called "Pride and Passion: The Italians in America". It dealt with how Italians immigrated here and how they lived their lives once they arrived. At one point I found myself tearing up as the narrator discussed how important Grandma was to the whole family.

As I get older, I have great nostalgia for an era that was filled with gobs of family and food. Sunday was the day you went to church and then went to Grandma and Grandpa's house for an eating marathon. The house would feel like it was going to burst from the din of enthusiastic conversations with intermittent exclamations of "mangia, mangia" from my grandmother.

No one went near the oven without permission. My grandmother's life centered on three things: family, food and Baby Jesus. If anyone looked upset, she would interrogate them until they told her what was wrong. But we all knew what her solution would be: "Eat something, don't forget me when I'm dead, and pray to Baby Jesus."

My grandfather would counter with, "Go have a glass of wine."

My favorite memories of those gatherings were how much fun they were. There were so many characters with so many stories, and I loved hearing their tales of woe, wisdom and wit. The food never stopped coming but neither did the drama and the comedy. I was often asked to imitate someone in the family or in films because it was noted early on that I had a specific talent in that area. Nothing felt better than watching all my relatives wiping tears from their eyes as they encouraged my antics. It was probably there that I began honing my theatrical skills.

I imagine many of you have had similar experiences no matter where your family comes from. It is up to us to pass on the stories and to create new ones for the next generation. There are so many distractions today that take us away from what is really important: our family and friends.

Eat, laugh, cry, share and have fun with them, for in the end, that's all that really matters.

Let's dump scientists, bring back grandmas

I just heard the most fabulous news. Spaghetti has been vindicated. The latest and greatest study on carbohydrates shows that an absence of carbs can create irritability, anger and hostility.

Wow!

Now we know what millions of Italians have known for years without having to study anything. I am convinced that my grandmother could have been an incredible scientist in the field of nutrition. She always seemed to know what foods to give to her family and friends.

Her daily diet consisted of coffee and day-old bread for breakfast. She always dunked the bread in the coffee, and she relished every bite.

Her lunch came late in the day and it always consisted of a little pasta with either broccoli, kale, or anything green.

Dinner was usually a bowl of soup and more day-old bread. She would splurge sometimes and have a little meat or chicken.

Her greatest joy came from eating a couple of sausages with more day-old bread. Her reason for eating hard bread was so her teeth wouldn't fall out. I never questioned her reasoning because none of her teeth had ever fallen out and she never had a cavity. When she died at ninety-three, she still had all her teeth.

One thing always remained a constant, and that was the daily dose of pasta. In fact, the whole family thrived on it.

I never asked for candy when I was a child, but I always begged for spaghetti, in any form. I especially loved it for breakfast, when it was left over from the night before. My grandmother would fry it until it was crispy around the edges and it was almost — but not quite — burned.

She was a wizard in the kitchen. I'm sure she could have made a tasty dish out of dirt. Every time I read about a new finding about food or the latest diet I think of this woman, who had no formal education beyond the third grade and who knew instinctively what we should all know: "All things in moderation."

I am always amazed at how many people seemed to become instantly seduced into believing a certain type of food is the reason behind their extra poundage. Yet the French and Italians continue to eat and enjoy delicious food without hysteria, so why can't we? We demonize and deify certain foods and have done so for quite some time. Our overwhelming need to control our food intake has backfired. The so-called illegal foods become more and more alluring and suddenly you find yourself thinking about how you are going to sneak a bowl of pasta, which you have been told is almost as bad as snorting coke.

I think it's time to get rid of the food police and put someone like my grandmother, Francesca, in charge of the American diet. I know we'd all be a lot happier.

Pets can teach us a few lessons about love

After my divorce, I got a cat from the local shelter. I had always wanted a pet but my ex-husband was allergic to cats and dogs and so we had a pet-free home. The cat I chose was a big, three-year-old domestic shorthair. I named him Studley.

I wrote about him in my column, and he became my buddy. When I had hip replacement surgery, he was ever-present. Unfortunately, Studley died. He had a heart attack right in my arms. I felt as though my own heart would break. Who would ever think that you could fall so madly in love with a cat? I'm sure millions do.

I know how many of you out there have pets and that you have loved and lost some. But I never had the experience. In fact, I was often amused at how my friends with pets would practically swoon with delight over their furry friends. Little did I know that I, too, would walk down that path?

I am very lucky to have people around me who love and care for me. They came to my rescue and said, "Don't wait, you need to go right back to the cat shelter and get another cat." I didn't think this was possible. Can we mend our hearts by attempting to replace one cat with another?

Although I was reluctant to find what I thought might be another Studley, I did so just to appease my friends. As we went from one shelter to the other, my mind kept telling me, "This is silly, just forget it. Why do you want to take the chance of being hurt again?"

Finally we landed in Duxbury, at a shelter run by some lovely women who dedicate themselves to our feline brothers and sisters. None of the cats appealed to me except one: a big ball of white fur with what looked like a black mask on his face and a big, black, furry tail. He kept sidling up to me and looking intently at me with a pair of gorgeous green eyes. Everyone said, "That's the one!"

I took him home thinking, "He's not Studley." And he wasn't! He had very strange habits, like suddenly charging me without warning. I often thought he had a multiple-personality disorder. One minute he was purring and the next; he was biting and madly twitching his tail. I thought, "This cat is nuts and he needs to go back where he came from." But my instincts told me to keep giving him love and attention and to wait to see what might happen as a result. Well, I'm glad to report that Mr. Boo has turned into the most loving, affectionate cat one could hope to have. He is always at my side and I must admit that I love him to pieces. It appears that we humans have great capacity to love, lose that which we love and love again. It certainly makes life worthwhile.

Be polite or suffer the silent treatment

Often we're rushing around so much that we become incredibly intolerant of others. Time has become a measurement of how much needs to get done, and life is a daily race.

Sadly, many of us live under the illusion that when we reach the finish line, we will feel relief. This becomes a daily ritual that, in and of itself, causes a great deal of stress and leaves us frustrated and unable to connect in a civilized manner.

The irony of this mindset is that the very opposite is true. If we slow down and take the time to be polite and considerate, we actually have more respect for ourselves. When we act more humane, our minds and bodies are freer to be more present and focused; therefore, we are more productive.

When I was a child, my grandmother spent hours teaching me manners. My mother worked, so it became Grandma's responsibility to create her ideal, dignified, gracious human being. Anything else would not be tolerated, and if she witnessed anything less, she would repeat over and over that I was acting like an animal.

"Don't chew with your mouth open." "Put your fork down when you're not eating." "Think before you speak." "Don't mumble."

These instructions, plus many more, had a dual purpose: They helped me function better in society, and they were a source of pride for her. To my grandmother, there was no greater sin than being ill-mannered; it brought disgrace upon her good name.

For that she reserved the ultimate punishment: silence. Silence from an elderly Sicilian grandmother can be compared to life imprisonment. An entire act accompanied the silence — big sighs, heavy walking while she prayed for your soul, and hand gestures similar to what the Roman emperors gave to those who were about to die.

Finally, my grandfather would intercede by yelling, "Basta" (enough). He was the only one who could end the punishment, aside from God.

Human survival is dependent on healthy relating. Interacting with people requires understanding, kindness, consideration, compassion and acknowledgment, which is what manners are all about.

The poet William Blake sums it up beautifully: "Everything that lives, Lives not alone, Nor for itself."

A wonderful Italian saying: At the table, one never grows old

I love Thanksgiving because it's all about food, family and friends. Some of my fondest memories are of Thanksgiving dinners with some of my relatives who are gone but not forgotten.

My grandmother could not just have a turkey with all the trimmings. She had to integrate some sausage and peppers, ravioli, and fried eggplant. Stuffing things was one of her greatest passions. If she could have, she would have stuffed a pea. It gave her great pleasure to see the surprise on people's faces when they bit into something and discovered something else inside it.

I'd watch her stern-looking face turn to one of glee as she waited for someone to ask her what she had used in her stuffing. Her answer was always ambiguous. After all, why would she reveal what made her unique? She needed and demanded the accolades her culinary audiences gave her.

Even I, who she often designated as her favorite granddaughter, was never privy to her secrets. If she had a cooking show, you can bet that she would have passed along all the wrong ingredients. Despite her secrecy, I was able to replicate many of her recipes by simply watching her and being her sous chef.

There is something wonderfully Italian about creating and sharing food; "A tavola non s'invecchia," which means, "At the table, one never grows old."

The memories from my childhood and beyond concerning food often sustain me when I am going through troubling times.

I have often cooked up a plate of spaghetti and covered it with my grandmother's recipe for her "little red sauce" and felt myself transported back to a feeling of comfort and calm. Much of what we hear today is about how many foods are bad for us. It has helped create a society that has an adversarial relationship with food.

We would be much better off if we paid attention to how much we ate. One of my favorite sayings is by Miss Piggy: "Never eat anything bigger than your head."

You might want to keep that in mind when you fill up your plate. But, more importantly, I hope you will spend your meals culling memories that you can savor in years to come and find delight in being grateful for the food and the people you are sharing it with.

From kids we learn there's still hope for us

In the past few weeks, the news coming out of Iraq has left me feeling very sad about human behavior. Not a day goes by without some new and startling information.

It is easy to fall prey to becoming jaded and cynical about the nature of man and where we are all headed. And so the other evening, I was given an incredible gift — a window of hope that all is not lost. I went to see my granddaughter, Erika, perform in the Plymouth Community Intermediate School production of *The King and I*. It was exquisite!

Oh, I'm sure you're thinking, "You're the grandmother. Of course you think it's great. She could butter a piece of bread and you'd applaud." Well, you're probably right. But dear readers, when I tell you this was superior in every way, I truly mean it. I have seen this production on Broadway and in the movies, and these kids were "right on". I was in awe of their ability to remember lines and songs flawlessly. The play was adapted to fit a shorter time frame but it was done so brilliantly that none of the storyline was lost. The sets were great, the costumes were wonderful and the kids came together as an ensemble.

You could sense that they were putting their whole heart and soul into the production. I was struck by the amount of time it must have taken to put this piece together. Not only did the students have to put their efforts into practicing and keeping up with their school work, but let us not discount the enormous sacrifice that it takes for teachers to add extra hours to their already overburdened schedules.

Day after day, we are assaulted with news that focuses on murder, war, robberies and abuse. We know that is the nature of blaring headlines. I have never seen a front page story that shouted, "School Play Delights All Who Attend".

"Don't be silly," you say. "How mundane. It wouldn't interest that many people."

Well, maybe it's time to put the stuff that makes you twitch on the back page and create a front page that makes you feel that the human race has some merit. I want to see and hear more about the greatness that surfaces every day because someone somewhere is doing something magnificent. Perhaps by becoming a witness to greatness, our own could come forth more readily.

As I watched the evening's performance, I felt proud to be an American in Plymouth, Mass., knowing that my tax dollars are helping to support a school system that has taken the time and effort to create what I thought was an amazing experience!

If my grandmother could see us now...

I think I've finally come to the place where I realize I'm starting to sound like my grandmother. Whenever new products or world events were brought to her attention, she would counter with a huge sigh and a prayer that she would not be around to witness the degradation and demise of society.

My grandmother was sure that canned tomato sauce was created by the worst faction of society: lazy people.

Who in their right mind would not crush their own tomatoes and add fresh basil and oregano from their garden?

And for that matter, who in their right mind would want to go to the moon, let alone walk on it? Didn't they have enough space to roam around right here?

When hot pants were hot, I bought a pair, along with a cool pair of boots and a snazzy see-through top. She took one look at me in my new outfit and asked when I was getting dressed. She also made it known in no uncertain terms that she did not bring me up to look like I belonged on a street corner.

When rock 'n roll music permeated the house, the Rosary beads and prayer books would come out, and invocations resounded throughout the house in hopes that the satanic sounds would be exorcised.

I am realizing that my own reactions to our modern-day society are starting to parallel my grandmother's. I am in awe of body piercings and wonder, what next? Will someone decide to put a lead pipe in his or her head and paint it so that it glows in the dark? And just how few clothes can we wear to entice and seduce people until we're actually just walking around butt-naked? Or will a time come when we're so sick of seeing everyone's private parts that we'll revert to wearing shrouds?

Will the likes of Frank Sinatra and Ella Fitzgerald ever return? They had names that sounded like regular people, and they had talent, not gimmicks. I admire a lot of the new talent, but it does make me laugh when I see them surrounded by a whole circus act.

I have an even more difficult time trying to decipher today's lyrics. But then my grandkids say, "You just don't get it." And they're right; I don't, and I don't want to.

I'm really trying to stay current, but part of me is quite nostalgic for a time when there wasn't always a need to look and act edgy. Well, enough of this gentle reminiscing. It's time for me to go buy a Harley, pierce my tongue, color my hair orange and get a tank top.

Save some of your love for people, not things

Our culture is permeated with the word "love". Celebrities set the tone for excessive kissy faces and multiple "love you, love you's every time they see one of their own, even though they might have trashed them in an interview. Commercials show people fondly caressing their iPods and cell phones while they ooze words of love.

Women love their bras, their hair products, their high heels and their skin products. Men are less effusive about showing love for things, although all you have to do is watch a man around his new car or a new gadget like a power saw to know he's in love.

I don't remember love being bandied about this way when I was growing up. My grandmother, who was somewhat stoic, doled out words of love occasionally to her favorite family members. I was fortunate to be one of them. She never gushed or threw her arms around me with great gusto. She always behaved as if she was giving you something she couldn't bear to part with. You knew you were special when Francesca whispered in your ear, "I love you."

Even my grandfather, who was much more demonstrative, rarely used the word "love" to describe his feelings. You could sense it and see it in his body language, but rarely did I hear him tell my grandmother that he loved or adored her. There were no cards given with flowery verbiage, or flowers sent on special occasions. Everyone just knew that everyone else respected and adored one another. It was an energy that was felt and admired.

I believe they had a love that many of us are missing in our lives because we have become slaves to a form of love that has been redefined by the media and the proponents of consumerism. We are forgetting what real love is. It is not a word to be bandied about to describe everything from brow tweezers to pizza. I realize that we are not going to omit these descriptions from our vocabularies, but they do speak more to the love of stuff than the love of each other. Perhaps we need to revisit, as a culture, why Herman Melville wrote: "We cannot live for ourselves alone. A thousand fibers connect us with our fellow man."

For our mental and physical well-being and in order to thrive and survive, we need to experience the love of being connected to someone else. Family and friends can supply this important function and so can a pet. We also can reach out and give our love to those in need beyond our borders. I truly believe that our world needs true love now more than ever. Make sure you bring it into your life on a daily basis. It will enrich you far more than you ever imagined and help to bring peace into the world.

Enduring can be a double-edged sword

I try to exercise whenever I can so I can keep myself agile enough to continue my career. This takes a great deal of endurance. "Endurance" is an interesting word. I have always associated it with being fit so you have lots of energy to do whatever you have to do. But I discovered another very interesting definition as I tried to distract myself from going bananas walking to nowhere on a treadmill in a gym in Iowa.

I got caught up watching an old black-and-white movie called "Night of the Iguana" with Richard Burton, Deborah Kerr and Ava Gardner. I saw this movie many moons ago when I was a young mother of three children. I never really got into it except to drool over Richard Burton and his mesmerizing voice. This time, however, I became totally involved with the dialogue because I had somehow reached a place in my life where it resonated with me.

In the movie, Burton plays an alcoholic minister who struggles with his demons every day. He is stuck with two women, played by Kerr and Gardner, one prim and proper, the other a woman who has seen it all and lets everybody know it. As he becomes more and more agitated, the women decide to tie him up in a hammock. He rants and raves as Kerr sits and gently tries to spoon-feed him a relaxing tea. As he calms down, he asks Kerr's character, whose persona rivals that of Mother Teresa, how she has handled her inner demons over the years. Her response to the question lingers with me still: "I endured," she answered.

In other words, she hung on as one would hang on to a life raft until the storm is over. If we were all to look at our lives, how many of us have endured to get through a crisis, and how many of us have endured too much because we didn't have the courage to do something differently? There's a fine line between the two.

Staying in a relationship that isn't working makes enduring feel like a prison sentence, while seeing someone you love through chemotherapy makes you feel protective and loving. You might want to look into what areas of your life you are enduring just because your guilt buttons have been pushed to the "stuck" position. Conversely, the situations that make you feel like enduring are feeding your soul. It could be the difference between feeling good about yourself or wishing someone would come to your aid and rid you of the energy vampires that are cramping your style.

Our pets can teach us a thing or two about humans

It's been more than a year since I got my cat, Mr. Boo, also known as Boo Bear and the Boomeister. As I write his aliases, I realize that I have totally lost my mind over this precious animal. When I am home from a road trip, he is constantly at my side. As I am typing this article, he is sprawled out on my desk, sound asleep. At night he sleeps at the foot of the bed, and sometimes he pads his way to the head of the bed and plops himself next to me for a ritualistic midnight petting session.

I lay there at 2 or 3 in the morning, thinking how nuts this is and yet, how poignant.

I would have killed for the same treatment from my ex-husband. Affection had to fit into a certain time frame, and the middle of the night was not part of the protocol.

What is it about love, attention, nurturing and affection that gets so easily put aside for those we love but that seems to come easily when it centers on a pet? The obvious answer is that animals demand nothing from us but shelter and food, some play time, and a pat on the head. They don't accuse or criticize us for not doing more, nor do they bring up past grievances to remind us of how we failed them. We can smell good or bad, be dressed to the nines or have on a sloppy T-shirt and sweats. The tail still wags, the purring continues and the greeting is always joyful. They never meet you at the door with a dour look on their face or reprimand you because you forgot to shut the hall light off before you left the house. Their love is always unconditional, their acceptance total.

We humans find this concept so difficult.

Perhaps it gets easier with age. I do find that I am able more often to let go of certain traits in people I love. My inner critic often jumped out of my mouth as I tried desperately to change what I considered to be traits unworthy of them.

Most of what I said went skyward. I assumed it went there because they always looked up and rolled their eyes. Sometimes they simply returned my criticism with some of their own. I'm sure neither one of us felt better.

If only animals would put on workshops for people on how to be better humans through pet psychology. I'm sure we might learn more patience, more acceptances, more joy in the simple things, but the most important lesson might be that we would learn to love and be loved for whom and what we are, not for what we think we should be.

Wouldn't that be just purrrrr-fect?

Wonderful memories last a lifetime

A lot of movies lately seem to be about magical kingdoms and other-worldly scenarios. Most of us love a mystical story with a happy ending. The ogre gets killed or skulks away with his tail between his legs, or he has an epiphany and becomes tender and caring. We all need to believe on some level that good will triumph over evil. We leave the theater uplifted and feeling "all's well that ends well".

Unfortunately, in our daily existence, we miss or have forgotten many magical moments and treasures because life takes on a life of its own. We all tend to get caught up in business, especially in these times when we can be *on* 24/7.

I remember my grandmother simply sitting in her chair mending socks for hours, with no distractions like a blaring TV or vibrating cell phone. She would look up periodically and make mention of how good the sauce smelled or to ask if I wanted some biscotti. Her intermissions from mending were always about eating.

Eating, however, was also done without distraction. She didn't mend and eat, because that would have been blasphemous.

I have much nostalgia for those moments.

I encourage you to share the magical moments of the past with your loved ones and friends. We have many treasures to give that cannot be bought. It will take more time than going shopping, but nothing can compare with passing on the treasures of the past.

I suggest you write about some of the wondrous and happy times you might have spent with parents, grandparents or siblings. Include pictures if you have them, or recipes. They can be funny or poignant.

So much of my career has been buoyed by stories I have shared about my Italian family. My grandmother often said to me: "Don't ever forget me." And I never have!

Some families may have their share of ogres, but more often than not, moments stand out that left wonderful impressions. Don't forget them! They cost nothing, but they can mean everything.

Made in the USA
Charleston, SC
16 December 2013